HOW TO BE A
WORLD-CLASS
CHRISTIAN

BECOMING PART OF GOD'S
GLOBAL KINGDOM

PAUL BORTHWICK

While this book is intended for the reader's personal enjoyment and profit, it's also designed for group study.

Use this excellent resource to ignite many—your family, your small group, your short-term mission teams, and even your church—into a lifestyle that is world focused and prepared to join in God's global plans.

Scriptures and discussion questions for group study are located at the end of each chapter.

HOW TO BE A
WORLD-CLASS
CHRISTIAN

BECOMING PART OF GOD'S
GLOBAL KINGDOM

PAUL BORTHWICK

WITH A FOREWORD BY

RICK WARREN

IVP Books

An imprint of InterVarsity Press
Downers Grove, Illinois

InterVarsity Press
P.O. Box 1400, Downers Grove, IL 60515-1426
World Wide Web: www.ivpress.com
E-mail: email@ivpress.com

InterVarsity Press® is the book-publishing division of InterVarsity Christian Fellowship/USA®, a movement of students and faculty active on campus at hundreds of universities, colleges and schools of nursing in the United States of America, and a member movement of the International Fellowship of Evangelical Students. For information about local and regional activities, write Public Relations Dept., InterVarsity Christian Fellowship/USA, 6400 Schroeder Rd., P.O. Box 7895, Madison, WI 53707-7895, or visit the IVCF website at <www.intervarsity.org>.

Originally published by Biblica.

Cover design: Nick Lee
Interior design: projectluz.com
Editorial team: Dana Bromley, Daniel Johnson

ISBN 978-0-8308-5680-0

Printed in the United States of America ∞

Cataloging-in-Publication Data is available through the Library of Congress.

P	17	16	15	14	13	12	11	10	9	8	7	6	5	4	3	2	1
Y	26	25	24	23	22	21	20	19	18	17	16	15	14	13	12		

Contents

FOREWORD
2009

You have a choice to make. As my friend Paul Borthwick clearly explains in this wonderful book, you will be either a *world-class* Christian or a *worldly* Christian.

God invites you to participate in the greatest, largest, most diverse, and most significant cause in history—his kingdom. History is *his story*. He's building his family for eternity. Nothing matters more, and nothing will last as long. From the Book of Revelation we know that God's global mission *will* be accomplished. Someday the Great Commission will be the Great Completion. In heaven, an enormous crowd of people from "every race, tribe, nation, and language" will one day stand before Jesus Christ to worship him (Revelation 7:9 CEV). Getting involved as a world-class Christian will allow you to experience a little of what heaven will be like—in advance.

When Jesus told his followers to "go into all the world and preach the Good News to everyone" (Mark 16:15 NLT), that small band of poor, Middle Eastern disciples was overwhelmed. Were they supposed to walk, or ride slow animals? That's all they had for transportation, and there were no ocean-crossing ships; so there were real physical barriers in going to the whole world.

Today we have airplanes, ships, trains, buses, and automobiles. It's a small world after all, and it's shrinking daily. You can fly across the ocean in a matter of *hours* and be home the next day if you need to be. The opportunities for normal, everyday Christians to become involved in short-term international missions are now literally limitless. Every corner of the world is available to you—just ask the travel industry. We have no excuse not to spread the good news.

And with phones, faxes, and the Internet, the world has gotten even smaller. Any believer with Internet access can personally communicate with people in virtually every country on earth. The whole world is at your fingertips!

Even many remote villages get e-mail, so you can now carry on *"e-vangelistic"* conversations with people on the other side of the world, without leaving your home! Never in history has it been easier to fulfill your commission to go to the whole world. The great barriers are no longer distance, cost, and transportation. The only barrier is the way we *think*.

If you want to be like Jesus, you must have a heart for the whole world. You can't be satisfied with just your family and friends coming to Christ. There are over 6 billion people on earth, and Jesus wants all his lost children found. Jesus said, "Only those who throw away their lives for my sake and for the sake of the Good News will ever know what it means to really live!" (Mark 8:35 LB). The Great Commission is *your* commission, and doing your part is the secret to living a life of significance. *How to Be a World-Class Christian* will launch you on that journey.

Rick Warren
Pastor, Saddleback Church
Author, *The Purpose-Driven Life*

Portions of this foreword are adapted from Day 38 of *The Purpose-Driven Life*.

FOREWORD
2000

If you've ever felt overwhelmed by the challenges of our world, both near and far, Paul Borthwick has some good news for you. He's reduced the enormous and complex needs of people next door and across the world into manageable chunks so that an individual, small group, Christian education class, or an entire church can get excited about personal involvement.

Paul knows the questions that caring Christians are asking about creative involvement with people outside the walls of the church. His answers are refreshing, and he has learned how to tailor suggestions to the gifts, interests, time, and commitment level of members of the body of Christ.

To the person who aspires to be a world-class Christian but says, "I don't know how to get started," Paul offers several practical "low-risk starters." For people with considerable ministry experience, he challenges them with a wide variety of "higher and wider risks" in "going global."

His challenge to meet the local needs of people as well as the challenges half a world away is remarkably balanced. He refuses to create any artificial dichotomies between global ministry and outreach right in the community.

Paul is not triumphal about American wealth or success in the cause of worldwide kingdom ministry, "knowing the Sovereign Judge . . . squelches our feelings of superiority toward any other people on earth." Yet, through dozens of creative, practical ministry suggestions, he does not downplay the strategic partnership of American Christians.

Finally, Paul reminds us of the unseen resources at our disposal and the unseen God whom we must trust for anything worthwhile to be accomplished. "Jesus did not command his disciples to run around in frenzied activity trying to meet all the needs. He commanded them to pray that the Lord of the harvest would act."

Borthwick quotes Paul Tournier, who said, "Life is an adventure directed by God." Here is a wide spectrum of exciting, God-given ministry handles for those who refuse to experience the adventures of life vicariously.

Robert A. Seiple
Founder, Institute for Global Engagement
Former president, World Vision USA
Author, *Ambassadors of Hope*

ACKNOWLEDGMENTS

I thank God for the world-class Christians he has surrounded me with over many years of following Jesus. My first twenty-two years in ministry, at Grace Chapel in Lexington, Massachusetts, introduced me to dozens of people who served as catalysts for my personal growth as well as sources for many of the ideas found in these pages.

Some of these catalysts are now deceased—Dan Dustin, Eliot Eames, Josephine Kennedy. They are dead, but their voices of encouragement still speak, stirring me to remember that one person, one couple, one family, and one church can indeed make a global difference on behalf of Christ and his kingdom.

Globally aware and involved friends over the years have spurred me onward. Christie and I continue to be inspired by the Anzivinos and their commitment to Moldova, the Longs and their dedication to international students, the Engelsens and their commitment to microenterprise development in the name of Christ.

Senior pastors with global vision—Gordon MacDonald, Howard Clark, and Bryan Wilkerson—have all played a part in the ongoing development of my own world-class vision. Others who have fueled my global vision include my students studying cross-cultural ministry at Gordon College and Gordon-Conwell Theological Seminary; Jane and Harold Overstreet and all of our associates at Development

Associates International; and Jim and Beth Tebbe and the leadership team of InterVarsity's Urbana Student Missions Conventions.

I mention all of these folks because becoming a globally aware and internationally involved Christian does not occur in isolation. We grow together as we inspire each other to love and serve others.

And most significant of all there is Christie. Without her dedication to the endeavor of world evangelization, my growth would have been stunted. She has gone with me to war zones such as Afghanistan, Sri Lanka, and the Middle East to encourage the Christians there. She has been my example of learning about other cultures and people through listening and observing. She has set the pace for simpler living; stimulated my learning about global issues; and endured, in our global travels together, everything from bedbugs to dysentery to bathroom faucets that spit insect larvae.

I dedicate this book to her.

Paul Borthwick
September 2008

WHY BE A WORLD-CLASS CHRISTIAN?

Once you decide to ask Jesus Christ to take control of your life,
involvement in world missions is no longer optional.

PETER WAGNER

We live in exciting times. Historians' veins pump with adrenaline when they observe the changes, events, developments, and growth in our world. As Marshall McLuhan predicted years ago, our world has become a "global village." Electronic communication, jet travel, international networks, and interdependent economies have simultaneously shrunk the world while vastly enlarging the amount of information we try to manage.

In the midst of this expanding base of information and the shrinking global picture, we find ourselves striving to live on a "world-class" scale. Multinational corporations attempt to compete in a global market by reaching the elite distinction of becoming "world-class." An airline described itself as "World-Class, Worldwide." Television and sports networks introduce us to "world-class" athletes, and concerts highlight the performances of "world-class" musicians.

The adjective "world-class" now describes automobiles, computer technology, hotels, foods, lifestyles, and even disasters.

Dr. Howard Foltz, founder of Accelerating International Mission Strategies (AIMS), writes, "What does it take to be world-class? Florence 'Flo-Jo' Joyner, the tough and flashy runner who won several medals at the 1988 Seoul Olympics, is a world-class athlete who breaks world records. World-class autos are those which forge a sales niche in the world market, so how would you describe a world-class Christian?"[1]

If the business, sports, and media worlds strive to compete on a "world-class" scale, what about the followers of Jesus Christ?[2] Should we too be aiming at world-class excellence in our obedience? Are we to try to relate to the contemporary world so that the Christian faith addresses world-class problems?

The obvious answer is YES! God has given us the privilege of living at one of the most exciting, unique junctures in human history. Through a worldwide community, modern technology, and unparalleled global resources, we in the church of Jesus Christ have the opportunity to interact as never before on a "world-class" scale.

God invites us to join his world-class action. How will we respond?

But How?

We respond with a resounding, "Yes, Lord, I want to get on board!" That is, until we start to picture the magnitude of earth's problems:

- More than 6 billion people live on earth at this writing (and increasing daily!).
- Perhaps one-third of these have never heard of the love of God through Jesus.
- Millions of kids are starving, homeless, and hopeless.

- Megacities—with populations of 10, 15, or even 20 million people—are overloaded with social, economic, spiritual, and logistical challenges.

We do not need to carry the descriptions too far. We all experience it—the phenomenon known as "compassion fatigue," the feeling of frustration that laments, "What possible difference could one person or family or church make?"

The challenge of world-class living overwhelms us—until we begin to reduce the task to manageable chunks. One person likened getting a world vision to eating a five-hundred-pound marshmallow: we know what needs to be done, but we simply have neither the confidence that we can do it nor any idea where to begin.

Welcome to a book about beginnings. If *How to Be a World-Class Christian* were a college class, it would be titled something like "Becoming a Globally Aware Christian 101." If it were a seminar, it might be titled "Local Living, Global Impact." The pages that follow are simple steps all of us can take to find our part in God's global action.

But first, let's make a few observations about motivation. What will keep us going as we tackle this immense task?

But Why?

With the myriad of challenges we face in our personal lives, we need to choose wisely how to invest our time. Is this global pursuit worthwhile? Even if we decide to start toward the world-class growth goal, what motivates us to endure?

Only a few of us will admit it, but we may be quietly asking, "What's in this for me? If I aspire toward 'world-classness,' how will I grow? Will the reward justify the effort?"

Without indulging our self-centeredness to excess, we find motivation as we observe the tangible results in the lives of those growing to be world-class Christians. Let's consider seven areas.

Stimulation

The media and entertainment worlds have convinced our generation that life is a spectator sport. Like Chauncy, the gardener in Peter Seller's film *Being There,* "We like to watch." We watch while superior athletes compete. We experience adventure vicariously through movie superheroes or Indiana Jones–like pioneers or James Bond–like international spies.

For followers of Christ, even our faith can become an experience in watching as motivational preachers or dynamic personalities talk or sing or preach to us. Some have become "pew potatoes"—watching rather than participating.

Getting involved in the global scene stirs us to action. As a graduate student, I had the privilege of traveling to Haiti on an "Exposure Trip" designed to show us several international ministries there. When contemplating the trip, I confronted my first obstacle: finances. Yet God miraculously made it possible for me to go. Then the next barrier came: I had never flown before, and I (who as a child vomited when being rocked) feared my motion sickness. God took care of me—even on the twelve-seater flight to southwest Haiti, where we had to "buzz" the grass runway to clear off the grazing cows.

Every day for seven days—whether meeting Haitian Christians or speaking through a translator for the first time, whether eating unusual food or confronting a tarantula in the bathroom—I learned afresh what it meant to trust God, especially in the face of my own powerlessness. The involvement in Haiti invigorated my faith.

Very few people have ever come to me for counsel on how to quiet down their personal faith; actually, I can remember no such request. Most of us look for ways to enliven our faith, not deaden it.

Growing as a globally aware Christian stimulates our faith to develop, even as aerating soil stimulates growth in plants. It stirs us up. The pursuit of becoming world-class launches us into a world where we must trust God. Whether it means praying for the funds needed for an international project or walking out to minister in an unfamiliar neighborhood, an outward orientation of our faith encourages us to trust God in direct and practical ways.

One participant on an educational/service project to Egypt wrote: "I think the greatest lesson I learned on this trip was how to deal with difficult situations. . . . I learned this lesson because, with the nature of the trip, one had to learn these lessons to endure the experience. The work was hard, conditions uncomfortable, and amenities barely adequate—but with God's help I could withstand this and grow in my faith through the experience."

Pursuing the world-class goal puts us personally into the action. Rather than experiencing life vicariously through those we watch, we move from being spectators to participants. Reaching out in what might be risky relationships or volunteering for sacrificial service moves us out of our comfort zone into the arena of dependence on Christ. And, like Peter on the water, when we step out in faith, Jesus meets us there!

Focus

Don observed his own ability to be swayed by cultural opinions and current trends. He concluded, "I am the disciple of the last man who spoke."

Don illustrates the tensions we all face regarding priorities, choices, and a clarified focus in our lives. Advertisements dictate to us what we must have to be acceptable—whether cars, clothes, vacations, or perfume. We follow the advice of a pluralistic world that dictates standards of success, but we find ourselves being torn apart. In one way or another, we fall prey to becoming cultural Christians rather than true disciples.

Tom Sine, futurist and consultant, writes: "We all seem to be trying to live the American Dream with a little Jesus overlay. We talk about the lordship of Christ, but our career comes first. Our house in the 'burbs comes first. Upscaling our lives comes first. Then, with whatever we have left, we try to follow Jesus."[3]

We need help in focusing our lives.

In spite of the magnitude, a global awareness helps us do just that. Alertness to the needs of others, concern for the broken people of our world, and ideas of how to respond practically give us a new sense of priorities. Rather than an unhealthy preoccupation with the question, "Am I fulfilled?" we find ourselves asking how we can help others—and, in so doing, we find the fulfillment we were looking for in the first place.

A businessman in the financial district of Boston told me that serving meals at a soup kitchen for Boston's homeless clarifies the meaning of his life. "It makes me see myself as a fellow-straggler with these people, and this helps me keep my world and my problems in perspective."

An older couple has dedicated over twenty years to raising awareness in their home church of the needs in the tiny country of Moldova (population roughly 3 million). They've organized short-term mission trips, built an ongoing partnership between Moldovan churches and their own, and coordinated in their home church an annual event that provides clothing and supplies to over five hundred Moldovan orphans. They describe their experience this way: "When we were younger, we dreamt about changing the world, but *the world* was too overwhelming. By getting involved in serving Moldova, we found a new focus for our lives. We might not be able to change the world, but we can help change the life of a child or a church or a village in Moldova. It's been amazingly rewarding, and it's invigorated our faith here at home."

Joy

Similar to the businessman cited above, the Lands family added perspective to their lives by serving the Thanksgiving meal at a shelter for the homeless. Rather than gorging themselves on the typical "I-ate-too-much, pass-the-Alka-Seltzer" Thanksgiving dinner, they decided to go out to serve. Their practical yet sacrificial service produced greater thankfulness than they had known on any previous Thanksgiving.

One of the teenage daughters reflected, "At first we thought we would feel more thankful because we would realize how much more we had than these people . . . but the greatest memory of the day for me is joy. These folks who seemed to have nothing could give and experience joy together. Sharing in their joyful simplicity taught us far more than we gave them."

Venturing out into our exciting, frightening, hurting world teaches us that Jesus-type joy is joy in the face of hardship, joy in spite of the surroundings. An outward focus puts us in touch with the joy that Paul the apostle had in jail when he wrote in his most joy-filled epistle: "Rejoice in the Lord always" (Philippians 4:4). And this joy keeps us going through the roller-coaster ride of life.

Relevance

A few years ago, I asked a number of unchurched people their opinions about Christians and Christianity: "Who would you say is the best example of Christianity, in the way it's supposed to be lived?"

A few said Billy Graham, because of his public integrity. But the vast majority answered, "Mother Teresa of Calcutta and the Sisters of Charity." Mother Teresa is now deceased, but her impact continues in some of the poorest urban areas of the world through the order she founded, the Sisters of Charity. The reason? "Because these sisters are the only ones we see treating poor people the way that Jesus would."

Nobody commented much about their theology, their nun's habit, or their relative obscurity (few of these nuns are recognized in the way that Mother Teresa was). The dominant feature of Mother

Teresa and her companions, in the minds of these secular people, was an active, demonstrated faith.

These comments reminded me of the rebuke attributed to the existentialist Nietzsche: "His disciples will have to look more saved if I am to believe in their Savior."

Growing as world-class Christians helps us "look more saved." When we explain that we spent our weekend helping insulate someone's home or serving at a nursing home, people may inquire about the faith that motivates such action. When we spend a vacation visiting missionary friends, people ask us about our experiences, which inevitably leads to a discussion of our beliefs.

World-class involvement builds credibility because we begin to take an interest in world-class issues—whether political, religious, or environmental. My wife, Christie, strives to address the gospel values to rain forest destruction in South America. In so doing, she's able to integrate her faith into issues raised by environmental activists.[4] One non-Christian man came to hear me preach because I gained credibility in his eyes by my travels into the Muslim world. Another man, who was nominally religious, decided to worship at a Bible-teaching church because the church sent a team to build homes with Habitat for Humanity. Others are attracted to Jesus because they see or hear or read about Christians caring for HIV/AIDS orphans, defending the rights of immigrants, or using their business skills to alleviate poverty.

An outward focus of our faith—integrated into our world and addressed to real needs and issues—establishes our witness of the mercy of Jesus as credible, demonstrable, and relevant. Our world needs to see followers of Christ who indeed love mercy and do justice (Micah 6:8).

In the ever-shrinking global village that God sends us into, the world is asking, "What type of neighbors will these Christians be?" When we dive into service and start participating in the demonstration of Jesus' love, people start paying attention.

Direction

Stephanie started growing as a world-class Christian several years ago. For her, that growth led to involvement with international students, most notably scholars from the People's Republic of China. Working together with several friends, she used her gift of hospitality to entertain, feed, and love dozens of Chinese visitors.

After a few years of this ministry, she decided to go to China for a visit. She took a leave of absence from her engineering firm and traveled for five weeks in China, staying with men and women whom she had befriended on their visits to the United States. But Stephanie's trip was so tough, including bronchitis and a stint in a Beijing hospital, I thought she would quit her ministry to the Chinese—or at least never travel again.

Quite the contrary! After her return, Stephanie made contact with the English Language Institute. She applied, was accepted and trained, and taught English at a technical school in Beijing. Having dedicated the rest of her life to China, Stephanie has learned Mandarin and now helps supervise and coordinate the efforts of other teachers. Reaching out to the world beyond her normal sphere of influence put Stephanie in a new position to hear God. Her firsthand involvement gave new direction to her life.

Not everyone gets so radically redirected. Some find new ways to use their skills to serve—such as Bob, a Boston architect. He heard that an urban mission needed help redesigning and refurbishing their building in order to house those in need. In his spare time, and at no cost to the mission, he used his architectural skills to design a new wing for the mission. In so doing, he saved them thousands of dollars while feeling the satisfaction of using his skills to help others.

Or consider Pat, who uses her teaching skills to tutor urban students once a week. In her time spent with students, she has built a new network of friends, developed a new appreciation for the city, and helped students' grades go from Fs to Bs.

When we get tired of chasing the "American dream" because we find it empty or dissatisfying, God says, "I have a better way: service on behalf of others." Jesus taught it: If you want to be great, become a servant; if you want to be first, then become last (Mark 10:43–45). Jesus taught us that, paradoxically, we gain by losing; we lead by serving; we find ourselves by giving ourselves away. In the process of serving, we find new purpose and direction for the skills, abilities, and resources he has given us.

Sneak Previews

Any major motion picture lures us out early to catch the sneak previews so that (I presume) we can be the first to describe the characters and plot to our friends.

God also invites us to a sneak preview. Through growth as world-class Christians, we have the unique opportunity of getting a sneak preview of heaven, where those from every nation, tribe, people, and language will worship Jesus together (Revelation 7:9).

As a participant in several of the Lausanne Congresses on World Evangelization, I have marveled at the opening and closing ceremonies, where representatives of more than two hundred countries—in national dress, some with flags, others with instruments—lead the celebration and singing. People from many races, tribes, languages, and countries gather to sing praise to Jesus, the Lamb of God who takes away the sins of the world. I've thought to myself, *Wow. This is what heaven will be like!*

In a microcosm, we can see similar previews of heaven by worshiping with believers from other countries, believers who worship in other languages, follow other traditions, and sing in different tones. Without traveling more than twenty miles, I can worship with brothers and sisters from Brazil, China, Laos, or Haiti. As I worship with them—with all of the cultural "dressing" their service might include—I develop an enlarged vision of the body of Christ. This in turn enlarges my vision for his world and my vision of who he is—the Lord of the universe, the hope of the world.[5]

Pleasure

Put simply, our efforts to grow as world-class Christians please God. He is pleased because in the process of growing we imitate Christ (Philippians 2:5–11)—serving without reciprocation. Every year, our church sends volunteers to serve in various ways on mission teams. At least once each summer someone is asked, "Well, who pays you to do this?"

The team member explains, "No one. Actually, we pay to be able to serve on the team."

The amazed inquirer inevitably responds, "You mean you pay to work?"

They pay to serve because they are following the example of Jesus, who paid (with his own life) for the opportunity to serve us—even while we were still spiritually dead in our sins (Romans 5:8).

Outward-focused serving pleases God because it puts us at his disposal to work in his "harvest field" (Matthew 9:36–38). Developing as a world-class disciple pleases God because, in so doing, we break out of the entrapments of cultural Christianity and open ourselves to see him with greater love and to serve him with renewed vigor.

You Are Invited—Do You Accept?

I feel hurt when I find out, after the fact, that my friends had a party and I was not invited. Whether by unintentional oversight or deliberate rejection, no one likes to be left out.

The good news is this: God invites us into his worldwide action! No one is left out. The magnificent, awesome task requires every Christian to participate. We cannot do it alone. But together, as we grow to be world-class Christians, the world-class church will get God's work—the Great Commission[6]—done.

David Bryant, founder of PROCLAIM HOPE, teaches that God's primary goal is not to get each of us into the Great Commission. His goal is to get the Great Commission into us! God invites us into his worldwide action in order to change our lives. As we jump in, it will make us more like Jesus and help us experience all that God has for us. Let's go for it!

Biblical Texts to Study

- Acts 17:1–10

- Matthew 9:35–38

- Matthew 28:18–20

Things to Talk About

- Peter Wagner has said, "Once you decide to ask Jesus Christ to take control of your life, involvement in world missions is no longer optional." Why is this so?

- Read 1 Thessalonians 1 and 2. How did Paul minister to the Thessalonians?

- What were his attitudes toward them?

- What were the results of Paul's ministry with them?

- What benefits did Paul personally experience by being a world-class Christian?

- What are other benefits of being a world-class Christian? Why are these benefits important?

- How can they motivate us to become more involved in missions around the world?

2

WHAT IS A WORLD-CLASS CHRISTIAN?

Anthropologists . . . explain that at our core is a basic view of reality—a worldview. That worldview determines who we are, what we value, and how we behave.

GORDON AESCHLIMAN

Back in my years as a youth pastor, I was invited to Youth Specialties' national convention as a seminar leader. The West Coast version of the convention that year took place in San Francisco. I anticipated the trip for months. As a native of the Northeast, I had never been to San Francisco, although travel brochures, television shows, and other travelers had enticed me many times. I admit that part of my reason for accepting the invitation to speak was the time it would give me to explore San Francisco.

The seminar was about five hours old when the room began to shake. It felt as if a gigantic underground train was passing directly below our room. People clambered toward the door. The earth was moving, and we ran out just in time to see the elevator shaft of the hotel across the street rip away from the building and collapse.

It took several minutes for us to realize that we had just survived the worst earthquake San Francisco and the Bay Area had experienced in many years. Within twelve hours, the seminar was canceled, and we were all scrambling for any flight that would take us out of town. My "tour" of San Francisco never occurred.

As I sat on the airplane en route back to Boston, I was impressed by the number of times I had heard the term *world-class* in the past thirty-six hours. I recorded them in my journal. I had flown on a world-class airline into a world-class city, stayed at a world-class hotel where they claimed to serve world-class cuisine. Then there was the world-class disaster that would receive world-class news coverage around the earth.

I concluded my journal entry by asking, "What does it mean to be 'world-class'?"

Contemporary Definitions

When I started challenging Christians with the term *world-class,* the responses were mixed. Some loved it, thinking that I was encouraging an excuse to live a lavish lifestyle, fly in private jets, and indulge in rich foods. Others were deeply disturbed because they felt that no Christian should care about the things our culture calls world-class.

There is no consensus on what this adjective means. For some, it means "able to compete with the finest athletes in the world." This is certainly the meaning when we call Olympic competitors "world-class athletes." In business, the term usually refers to the ability to compete in a global economy, so a hotel chain or an airline advertises itself as "world-class."

World-class might mean "lofty," as was used in a *Reader's Digest* note advocating unstructured time that allowed one to think "world-class thoughts." It could simply mean "international," such as the label on a salad dressing mix that described the ingredients as "world-class spices." It may be used to set something apart from the average or mundane, as in the "world-class wardrobe" of some billionaire.

Any of these definitions could carry over with meaning to followers of Jesus Christ. We should aspire to be relevant on a worldwide scale, able to hold our own in discussions about world events, concerned about a faith that is truly international, and committed to being above the average in all our endeavors. But there is more.

The Definition for Followers of Jesus

A brochure came in the mail, inviting our investment in international stocks. On the cover was a map of the earth, but all countries had been deleted except the United States, which had been expanded to cover all of the global landmass. The caption read, "Because the World Doesn't Look Like This, Neither Should Your Investment Portfolio." Inside, the advertisers tried to convince us that an international, interdependent world demanded world-class investing in both foreign and domestic accounts.

The caption stirred my thinking about us as followers of Jesus Christ. Because the world does not look like just the United States, neither should our world vision. Because the world is much larger than U.S. culture, our prayers should be larger than just our normal sphere of influence. Because God is God of all nations, we dare not imply that he somehow belongs exclusively to ours. He calls us to be world-class Christians.

But what does that mean? Consider this definition of a world-class disciple of Jesus Christ: "A world-class Christian is one whose *lifestyle and obedience* are *compatible,* in *cooperation,* and *in accord* with what God is doing and wants to do *in our world*."

Let's evaluate the key words.

A World-Class Christian: Lifestyle and Obedience

We are not talking about some compartment of faith that affects only our concepts and perspectives. Trying to obey Jesus affects every part of our lifestyle. To borrow the analogy from Robert Boyd Munger's *My Heart, Christ's Home,* if our lives were a house, then each room would represent some specific aspect of our lives. Our kitchen would represent our appetites, our bedroom our sexuality, our recreation room our leisure, and our closets the things we keep hidden from outsiders.

When we come to Jesus, he asks for entrance into every room. If he is Lord of our lives, we cannot be satisfied to keep him in the sterile hospitality of the living room. He wants free rein of the house.

Peter's encounter with Cornelius, the God-fearing Gentile of Acts 10, illustrates God's ability to break into our closed "rooms" so that we might submit totally to his control. In Peter's worldview, excluding Gentiles from the gospel was legitimate. As a member of the chosen people of Israel, Peter could assume that the Messiah Jesus had come for only his people. But God broke through, using a repeated dream. When Peter was obedient, he realized that "God does not show favoritism but accepts men from every nation who fear him and do what is right" (Acts 10:34–35). When Peter allowed the Holy Spirit to have free rein, his world vision was enlarged.

My friend Marion illustrates an obedient lifestyle in another way. As she approached retirement, she could have followed the cultural norm of keeping those years of rest to herself. She might have thought, *I've had a tough life. I'm a widow. I've raised my kids as an urban, African-American single mom. I've worked long and hard for the benefits of retirement; I deserve a few years in the sun.* Instead, she let Jesus into every "room" of her life, including the room called "retirement" or "entitled rest."

Marion committed her retirement years to the Lord's service, including her years of accumulated experience as a nutritionist supervising the mass production of healthy meals, first at a hospital and later at a military compound. After two months of retirement from the food service industry, at age sixty-seven, Marion departed for a children's orphanage in Haiti. She served there for five months, training people to produce healthy meals for the children. When she arrived, they were feeding six hundred children per week; by the time she departed, her skills and knowledge of food technology had enabled them to feed two thousand children per week.

Several years ago, I had the chance to preach at Marion's funeral. She died at age eighty-five. After eighteen years of retirement and over forty trips to Haiti (forty!), Marion had spent plenty of time in the sun—but not for leisure. She used that time to establish Hope for the Children of Haiti, an organization committed to care for and feed hundreds of children in that economically troubled country. The ministry has built a school for children who otherwise would have no opportunity to gain an education.

Through her Christian lifestyle and obedience, Marion influenced dozens of others to go to Haiti to offer some sort of service. Now, her dream being carried on by Haitian pastors and church leaders, hundreds of children have had nutritious meals and a quality education. Her obedience helped give these children of poverty a brighter hope for the future.

A World-Class Christian: A Compatible Lifestyle

As Christie and I were wrapping up our day at Walt Disney World, she decided to take a few more pictures. I asked if I could wait for her on the benches at the end of "Main Street USA." As I rested in this re-created town square, which was supposed to be an image of average American life, I started listening to the conversations around me. One exhausted family argued with each other in

Spanish. Another family spoke German, and others conversed in Japanese. Within about twenty minutes, I heard six languages being spoken.

The experience reflects real life. On "Main Street USA," the multicultural dynamic of our modern world was being played out. The image stuck in my mind as a picture of the ethnically diverse, internationalized world into which we are called. Even if we live in places that were once shrines to Americana, they are now pictures of the global village. This is where we strive to be compatible with what God wants to do through us.

The dictionary defines *compatible* as "existing together in harmony." World-class Christians desire their lives to be in total harmony with God's purposes for his world. In other words, they want to find themselves in line with his will.

Jonah illustrates one who, at first, resisted being "compatible" with God's purposes. He ran in the opposite direction from God, but through some gentle persuasion by God's sovereign intervention, Jonah turned around. He decided (somewhat by force, I suppose) that being in harmony with God's purposes was better than running.

But Jonah is an example for all of us. When I read a futurist's prediction that the world's economy cannot support the current affluent lifestyle of the United States, I would rather run like Jonah than ask hard questions about what needs to be cut out of my lifestyle to be more in harmony with God's worldwide purposes.

The world-class Christian is willing to wrestle not only with what it means to be compatible with God's purposes but also with what it means to live in harmony with our brothers and sisters in Christ around the world. As we grow to understand what God is doing in the world, we cannot help but be challenged by our fellow believers in the non-Western world about our lifestyles, our commitment, and our zeal.

A World-Class Christian: In Cooperation with God

When Christie and I get into a canoe, we are good candidates for an entry in *America's Funniest Home Videos*. If we don't tip over, we row in circles, or we simply swamp the canoe slowly. Even though we've been told what we do wrong, we struggle to work together for effective forward progress.

Canoeing dramatically illustrates the need to work together. If she rows one way and I another, we go in circles. If we do not balance our weight, the canoe tips over. To get the canoe to do what it's supposed to do, we need to work cooperatively.

In the same way, to accomplish what God intends for us in his world, we must work cooperatively with him and with each other. This means basic obedience to the truths revealed in his Word, but it also means a radical willingness to turn away from aspects of our culture that may be acceptable in popular opinion but that "row" counter to the purposes of God.

Peter did this when he reached out to the Gentiles (Acts 10), engaging himself in a ministry that his culture called unclean but God declared clean. Jesus also cooperated with the purposes of God by reaching out to lost, lonely, rejected sinners. To be a friend of tax collectors and prostitutes was more important to him than popular opinion, because he was committed first to declaring the mercy of God.

Ananias was perhaps the most dramatic biblical "cooperator" of all (Acts 9). We know only that he was a "disciple in Damascus." God calls him to go minister to Saul, the terrorizing fanatic of the Pharisees who had overseen the stoning of Stephen and was presently on a rampage against the church.

Ananias voices his concerns (Acts 9:13–14), but the Lord says, "Go!" Ananias obeys, takes his life in his hands, and enters the house where Saul is staying. Cooperating with God's purposes took priority, even over his own safety. His opening words reveal the depth of his obedience: "Brother Saul" (Acts 9:17). It was as if a Jew said to a Nazi, "Brother." If we have never faced an enemy who has done us physical or emotional harm, we cannot fathom the depth of emotion that must have filled Ananias. He faces a man whom he had probably prayed against only days earlier, and he says, "Brother!" Actions of the past dissipate like smoke, and Ananias opens his arms to welcome Saul into God's family. Ananias knew what it was to keep his own feelings secondary in exchange for cooperating with the higher purposes of God.

Cooperating with God may not be as drastic as Ananias experienced, but we're still called to pursue God's higher purposes—even when we don't understand what God is doing. There was, in the 1980s, an extreme anti-USSR, anticommunist sentiment in the United States and, correspondingly, in many churches. In the summer of 1989, a sixth-grade teacher from a Christian school in Maryland used her summer vacation to visit what was then East Germany. The sight of the Berlin Wall, which separated East from West Germany, overwhelmed her because of the oppression it represented. When she returned that September to teach in her sixth-grade class, she asked her students every day to join her in prayer for the leaders of East Germany and for political and religious freedom in that country.

These children joined in prayer, cooperating with God through their requests and heartfelt cries for oppressed people. Only a few months later, against seemingly insurmountable obstacles, the Berlin Wall began to be dismantled, and East Germany gained its political and religious freedom. The boys and girls of that sixth-grade class exulted with an amazing sense of having cooperated in prayer together with the purposes of God.

A World-Class Christian: In Accord with God

I mentioned earlier the results of my informal survey about outstanding Christians. Almost without exception, Mother Teresa and her Sisters of Charity stood out in people's minds. Why? Because these servants live their lives in accord with what God wants to do in the world. Their treatment of the poor renders their faith credible. Their actions speak louder than their words. And their lifestyles preach the love they profess to believe.

To be credible is to be genuine. James exhorts us toward credibility when he tells us "faith without works is dead" (James 2:26 NASB). He writes, "Suppose a brother or sister is without clothes and daily food. If one of you says to him, 'Go, I wish you well; keep warm and well fed,' but does nothing about his physical needs, what good is it?" (James 2:15–16).

It's far better to document our faith by works than to have faith alone (James 2:18); even the devils have a semblance of faith (James 2:19). James exhorts us to live a credible, demonstrated faith.

The apostle John reiterates the point as he defines love based on our demonstrated acts of mercy toward those in need: "If anyone has material possessions and sees his brother in need but has no pity on him, how can the love of God be in him? Dear children, let us not love with words or tongue but with actions and in truth" (1 John 3:17–18). The world-class Christian is committed to growing toward a credible demonstration of faith "with actions and in truth."

Even Jesus demonstrated his credibility by his outward good works. When the disciples of John the Baptist asked for proof of Jesus' messiahship, Jesus responded by highlighting his treatment of broken people: "The blind receive sight, the lame walk, those who have leprosy are cured, the deaf hear, the dead are raised, and the good news is preached to the poor" (Matthew 11:5).

Our world desperately needs Christians who live in accord with God's will and demonstrate in their lives credible faith. Consider Chuck Colson, founder of Prison Fellowship. Perhaps the reason he has maintained such high respect in our world has little to do with his books, his radio commentaries, or his speaking engagements. Instead, his life consistently demonstrates his affinity for and commitment to prisoners—outcasts in every society. Referring to Colson, an inmate in Latin America said, "Anyone who will come into this stinking prison and share his food with me is worth listening to." Credibility provides the foundation for effective witness.

A World-Class Christian: In Our World

A pocket-sized book sits on my bookshelf. The cover promises that it contains a "compact guide to the Christian life." But when I scan the pages, I discover to my chagrin that there is no reference in the 228 pages to a Christian's commitment to be world minded, globally aware, or outreach oriented. Sadly, it reflects the attitudes of many who say, "Well, there are so many needs right here at home that we cannot think beyond our own worlds."

In contrast to such a narrow view, Gordon Aeschliman, author and former editor of *World Christian* magazine, describes the globalized world in which we live:

> In a village a thousand miles up the Amazon, people are reading the French-owned magazine *Elle* and the U.S.-produced *Better Homes and Gardens*. Guatemalans are ordering chicken chow mein, American youth are wearing Russian designer jeans, the Japanese are displaying their latest cuts at top Paris fashion shows, the French are eating Big Macs, the world is doing the lambada, and Japanese Ninja Turtles have given Batman the boot.[1]

In such an internationalized world, even a compact guide to the Christian life must include a global perspective. Our world-class commitment is to the "ends of the earth" (Acts 1:8), not just the end of the street or the extent of our Zip Code. God calls us out of our church pews and beyond our own comfort zones into other cultures, where we may confront differing worldviews and varying understandings of religion. Like the people of Israel, we follow the Lord of the universe, who reminds us that it is "too small a thing" for us to be preoccupied with ourselves; instead, his plan is to make us a "light" for those outside the gospel so that "you may bring my salvation to the ends of the earth" (Isaiah 49:6).

Several years ago, while speaking at a nearby seminary, John Stott told the story of a tiny church in rural England that he attended while on a study leave. He worshiped with them every Sunday, participated in their fellowship, and heard their discussions. He related his dismay when, week after week, the pastor would preach about issues facing the village, pray about concerns in the church, and discuss decisions related only to their congregation. "I came to the conclusion," Stott observed, "that these people worship a village God."

Our God is not some sort of "village God," existing for our concerns alone and isolated to our worlds. He is the Lord of the universe, the God to whom all will give an account, the Savior who reaches out through his church to all who need to know his love, regardless of ethnic background, economic standing, or geographic location.

A world-class perspective remembers to focus on a global God who calls us onto his team.

Lessons from a World-Class Disaster

From a world-class disaster in a world-class city, the question arises: What does it mean to be world-class? For followers of Jesus, it means abandoning self to him and his purposes. It means giving ourselves to his world so that people may see our lives as living illustrations of the gospel. It means being recognized as having been with Jesus (Acts 4:13), because his imprint marks our lifestyles and actions.

In *The Grapes of Wrath*, John Steinbeck summarizes the lives of several people with these tragic words: "When they died, it was as if they had never lived." They had no impact, left no legacy, and affected no lives.

In contrast, the teacher in the popular movie *Dead Poet's Society* challenged his students with the words *carpe diem*—"seize the day." He stirred them to make their lives extraordinary: "The powerful play [of life] goes on, and you may contribute a verse." The spirit of such words grips us. We all want to make a difference. We all want to offer a contribution to God's worldwide purposes.

We fear Steinbeck's tragic epitaph, but the solution to our fears is found in Jesus. As we give ourselves to be his world-class followers, we can be his agents of change in our broken world. We can be his world-class disciples.

Biblical Texts to Study

- Scriptures regarding Jesus
  Matthew 11:1–6

  Mark 2:13–17

  Luke 7:36–50

  Acts 10:38

- Scripture regarding Ananias and Barnabas
  Acts 9:1–31

- Scripture regarding Peter
  Acts 10:1–48

Things to Talk About

• Referencing the Scriptures above, how did Jesus, Ananias, Barnabas, and Peter demonstrate that they were world-class believers?

• What obstacles did each have to overcome in living as a world-class Christian? How did they do so?

• What were the results of their ministries?

• Read James 2:15–26 and 1 John 3:17–18. Why is our obedience to these passages important in becoming world-class believers?

• Why are good works crucial to a world-class outlook?

• Gordon Aeschliman writes, "Anthropologists . . . explain that at our core is a basic view of reality—a worldview. That worldview determines who we are, what we value, and how we behave." What steps will you begin taking to more closely align your worldview with God's?

3

THE SCRIPTURES AND THE SAINTS

Our God is a missionary God.

JOHN STOTT

Those who follow the great stories of NCAA basketball and the "March Madness" competition remember the tragic story of Hank Gathers. This young man, a promising center on the Loyola Marymount University basketball team, died during a game from complications of an irregular heartbeat. The grief of the team and the school spread across the country.

A short while after his death, the Loyola Marymount team entered the NCAA tournament, but they were considered one of the lesser teams, and experts predicted they would be eliminated in the first competition. The teammates dedicated their playing time to their fallen comrade, Hank. One player, Hank's best friend, shot his first free throw each game left-handed—Hank's shooting hand. Emotions ran high for the team and their fans.

The Loyola Marymount team, playing without their star center, won their first game in the NCAA tournament, and the emotions intensified. The players spoke openly of winning the tournament for Hank. In the second round of play, they won again, dethroning the past year's champion. In a third game, they defeated a team that possessed superior talent. The sports commentators turned their attention to one repeated question, "How far can this emotion take them?"

The answer came quickly. The Loyola Marymount team was soundly defeated in the next round by the team that would eventually win the tournament. Emotion could not sustain them.

The scene could be repeated in many of our lives. In the face of death—more specifically, the deaths of many people in our world who suffered in hardship, starvation, and ignorance of the gospel—we fill up with emotion. The image of thousands or millions perishing without Christ can stir our emotions deeply. Such a vision can lead to zeal, commitment to the cause of Christ, and an overwhelming desire to win the spiritual battle.

But the commentators who watch our emotional zeal step back and ask, "How far will this emotion take them?" And—like the Loyola Marymount team—we find out that emotion is not enough. With overwhelming odds and our own feelings of helplessness, emotion cannot sustain us. We need two foundation stones in order to sustain our commitment to grow as world-class Christians: the Scriptures and the saints.

The Biblical Perspective

Scripture—God's Word—is the first foundation stone we need. Oswald Chambers, writer of the devotional classic *My Utmost for His Highest,* reminds us that "the basis of missionary appeals is the authority of Jesus Christ, not the needs of the heathen."[1] In other words, we commit ourselves to grow as world-class Christians because Jesus says to in his Word, not because it's the popular or emotionally compelling thing to do.

How many times have we seen media reports turn the world's attention toward the plight of suffering people: the oppressed victims of an attempted genocide; survivors of an earthquake or flood or tsunami; or famine-ravaged people in a war zone. Fund-raising events commence. Churches take special offerings. A rock star organizes a concert that successfully raises millions of dollars to help alleviate the suffering.

However, eighteen months after the fundraiser, the offering, or the concert, attentions have turned elsewhere. The emotional appeal of the need in [you name the location—Sudan? Myanmar? Bangladesh?] has dissipated. And projects initiated during the "boom" of giving were abandoned, half-completed because the money, like the soil of a drought-ravaged country, had dried up.

Why? Because emotions cannot sustain the mission. They are necessary and operate effectively as catalysts, but they are not enough. Our vision for being involved as world-class Christians must be built on the sure foundation of God's Word. Our global commitment emanates out of the heart of God, not out of some popular fad.

We build our vision and sustained involvement on the purposes of God as revealed in his Word.

Genesis

Genesis introduces us to the global God, the Creator of the ends of the earth. The first family is commanded to be fruitful, multiply, and fill the earth. God's desire is that humanity, his highest creation, would enjoy and fill the earth, over which he reigns as Lord.

Genesis also teaches us of the origin of evil in our world—an independent spirit that led to sin. But once more, God shows himself to be the divine pursuer, looking for fallen mankind and seeking to restore Adam and Eve to fellowship with himself.

We also meet in Genesis the world-class father of faith—Abraham. We learn that God desires to bless all the nations of the earth through him. Abraham, the prototypical missionary, is sent across land and across cultures that he might be a blessing to all people. As Genesis concludes, Abraham's great-grandson Joseph continues the universal blessing theme. Through Joseph's life, Egypt, the tribes of Israel, and indeed "many lives" (Genesis 50:20) are saved.

The Law

The Law (found in Exodus, Leviticus, Numbers, and Deuteronomy) teaches God's standards of behavior in a broken and sin-filled world. The people of Israel are the primary recipients of this Law. But recurrent throughout the laws that govern relationships is God's expressed desire to show kindness and mercy toward the poor, the disenfranchised, the weak, and the "outsider."[2]

The Law provides our biblical basis for reaching out to displaced and defenseless people, such as the homeless, the alien, the refugee, and the international student. Even in this section of the Scriptures that many of us regard as harsh and even irrelevant to our times, God reveals his heart for the hurting and lonely and broken.

The Books of History

The Books of History open our eyes to God's people in action—marching forward in conquest for his purposes and reaching out in mercy to those outside of the chosen people.

While we abhor the violence in these books and do not always understand God's purposes in the conquests, we nevertheless see his people marching forward. Countless pioneers, called to other cultures to spread the message of God's love, have gained courage from God's promise to Joshua: "I will give you every place where you set your foot" (Joshua 1:3).

In the Books of History, we learn of Naaman the Syrian, Rahab the harlot, and Ruth the devoted daughter-in-law of Naomi, all Gentiles but nonetheless illustrations of faith. The Books of History teach us of our call into the world, even as we see the victories and failures of those who have gone before us.

The Psalms

The Psalms enlarge our vision of worship as they turn our attention upward to the God of all nations. They exhort us to "declare his glory among the nations" (Psalm 96:3), and they remind us that "the heavens declare the glory of God" (Psalm 19:1).

The Psalms keep us from fretful anxiety about the plight of our world, commanding us to "be still, and know that I am God; I will be exalted among the nations, I will be exalted in the earth" (Psalm 46:10). Amy Carmichael found reassurance in this verse as she faced the staggering hardships of India from without and personal suffering from within. Leading her ministry for many years from her sickbed, she had only two pictures in her room: one framed the words "Be still," and the other read, "I know." The Psalms gave her calm assurance that the sovereign God would lead as her shepherd, even through the valley of the shadow of death.

The Psalms teach us that we serve as his agents in the earth and that "all the ends of the earth will fear him" (Psalm 67:7). These words of worship give us perspective. God is guiding the nations of the earth (Psalm 67:4), ruling forever by his power and watching over all of the peoples of the earth (Psalm 66:7). We cannot go wrong if we are submitted to him.

The Prophets

The Prophets speak the oracles of God, calling the people of faith back from their sin and directing them to be the light of revelation to the Gentiles and to all nations as they bring his salvation to the ends of the earth (Isaiah 49:6). In the Prophets, men of faith exhort the people of Israel to move out of their lives of comfort and into outreach and ministry.

The Prophets keep the vision of global revival in front of the people, who faced captivity and suffering, with both Isaiah and Habakkuk predicting the day when the earth would be full of the knowledge of the Lord, even as the waters cover the sea (Isaiah 11:9; Habakkuk 2:14). The Prophets direct us toward the coming Messiah, the One who would come to "proclaim peace to the nations" and establish his rule "from the [Euphrates] to the ends of the earth" (Zechariah 9:10).

The Gospels

In the New Testament, *the Gospels* introduce us to the promised Messiah arriving in humility. His first worshipers represent the breadth of his reign: They are not only the economic/social outcasts (the shepherds) along with the aged (Simeon and Anna), but they are also the royalty (the foreign kings who came from the East; that is, the first non-Gentile worshipers of Jesus).

By his coming, Jesus set the precedent for servanthood and love for the lowly:

> From golden streets and angel choirs,
> To dirt floors and lowing cattle
> Jesus emptied Himself
> That we might be full.[3]

The Lamb of God arrives at the start of the Gospels, he lives out his divine purpose, and he purchases salvation through his death and resurrection for any in the world who believe on him (John 3:16). Then, after demonstrating his power over death, he commands his followers to take the good news of salvation to all people, to preach repentance, to make disciples, and to openly identify themselves with their Lord.[4]

The Book of Acts

The Book of Acts illustrates the early church carrying out Jesus' mandate. The promised power of the Holy Spirit comes on them, and the witness begins. Starting to obey Acts 1:8, they declare the gospel boldly in Jerusalem, but it takes some persecution to get them out into Judea and Samaria (Acts 8:1).

Gradually, the ethnocentric spirit of Christianity as a Jewish sect is exchanged for the glorious diversity of an Ethiopian, the Samaritans, and even Gentiles entering the family of faith. With the entry of the gospel to the Gentiles, we meet Paul the apostle, who commences the spread of the gospel to the "ends of the earth."

The work of the Spirit within the people of Christ drove them outward. They simply could not stop speaking about what they had seen and heard (Acts 4:20).

The Epistles

The Epistles, written to churches planted by first-century missionaries, establish the fledgling church in faith and doctrine so that they could in turn proclaim the gospel to others. Because the churches turned outward, even in their hardships, their faith became known everywhere (1 Thessalonians 1:8).

The Epistle writers keep the vision of the worldwide gospel before their readers. Paul reminds the Romans of his aspiration to proclaim Christ where he had never been preached (Romans 15:20), and he instructs Timothy concerning God's desire for all to be saved and come to know the truth (1 Timothy 2:4).

Peter develops this same theme (2 Peter 3:9) and encourages his readers to stand strong in solidarity with their brothers throughout the world (1 Peter 5:9). James calls for genuine religion to be demonstrated by care for widows and orphans (James 1:27), and John exhorts his readers not only to speak of love but also to demonstrate love (1 John 3:18).

The writers of the Epistles wanted their readers (including us!) to be established firmly in the faith that should be proclaimed worldwide. They wrote to affirm our election in Jesus Christ, understanding that this would lead to "the destruction of our prejudices and our parochial notions and our patriotisms; we are turned into servants of God's own purpose. [We come to realize that] the whole human race was created to glorify God and enjoy him forever."[5]

The Book of Revelation

The Book of Revelation consummates the history started in God's creation in Genesis. In contrast to the city of Cain, which was established out of rebellion and sin, we are ushered into the city of God, the place where there is no need for light because God himself is the light.

At the throne of the Lamb of God, a great throng—those who have come to love Jesus Christ—worship and adore the global God. These people, from every nation, tribe, people, and language (Revelation 7:9), believe because of the witnesses sent to the ends of the earth. Their linguistic and cultural differences melt away in insignificance as they join in a chorus of praise.

In the following summary, John Stott reminds us that the Bible is the foundation for pursuing our commitment to the global cause of Christ.

> Without the Bible, world evangelization is impossible. For without the Bible, we have no Gospel to take to the nations, no warrant to take it to them, no idea of how to set about the task, and no hope of any success. It is the Bible that gives us the mandate, the message, the model, and the power we need for world evangelization. So let us seek to repossess it by diligent study and meditation. Let's heed its summons, grasp its message, follow its directions, and trust its power. Let's lift up our voices and make it known.[6]

The Historical Precedent

First-century believers followed Christ's commission simply in obedience to his Word. We, too, have his Word as the foundation of our commitment. But we also have a second foundation stone: the inspiration of the saints.

Saints who have gone before us and saints living today give us impetus to persevere. We do not operate in isolation. We have what the writer of Hebrews calls a "great cloud of witnesses" (Hebrews 12:1), sitting in the heavenly grandstand, cheering us on as we run our portion of the race for God's glory.

Heroes from the Past Cheer Us On

When we flag in our zeal, we can turn to the inspiring life of William Borden of Yale.[7] This heir to a family fortune sacrificed it all because of his commitment to the worldwide purposes of God. After donating thousands of dollars to the missionary endeavor, Borden went out as a member of the Student Volunteer Movement in an effort to reach Muslims. After only four months in Egypt, he contracted cerebral meningitis and died at age twenty-five. In spite of what appears from a human vantage point to be a tragically premature death, Borden cheers us on with his view of life, found in these words he inscribed in the flyleaf of his Bible:

> NO RESERVE.
> NO RETREAT.
> NO REGRETS.

We find courage from his example to continue without turning back.

In another section of that great grandstand sits Amy Carmichael, founder of the Dohnavur Fellowship in India. As we think of the pain we incur running our race of faith, Amy shouts out, "Hast thou no scar?" We remember her example of enduring great loneliness and physical burden in her last twenty years of ministry to temple prostitutes in India. We remember the poem in which she exhorts us with the voice of Jesus to persevere in spite of physical hardship:

But as the Master shall the servant be,
And pierced are the feet that follow me.
Can he have followed far
Who has no wound, no scar?

As we round another turn, we again contemplate quitting the race. But we encounter Lott Carey, the first black missionary sent from North America. Here we meet a man who was born into slavery, a world that told him he was less than a human. But Lott listened to God, not to people. He bought his freedom in 1813 and sailed to West Africa. Before departing, he said to his friends: "I am about to leave you; and expect to see your faces no more. I long to preach to the poor Africans the way of life and salvation. I don't know what may befall me, or whether I may find a grave in the ocean, or among the savage men, or more savage wild beasts, on the Coast of Africa; nor am I anxious what may become of me. I feel it my duty to go."[8]

Heroes of the Present Also Motivate Us

Chet Bitterman, a Christian martyr of the twentieth century, provides us with the encouragement we need to persevere in our growth toward being world-class Christians. His life and sacrifice remind us of God's sovereign purposes, accomplished even through pain and hardship. An aspiring Wycliffe Bible translator, Bitterman desired to serve in Malaysia. But because of the need for translators in Colombia, he instead, in 1981, traveled there to serve. Early in his time in Colombia, he was sent to the capital for gallbladder surgery. While awaiting surgery, he was mistakenly kidnapped by terrorists and held for forty-eight days—before being shot through the heart.

A tragedy? Some think so. But consider this: Because of the highly publicized news of Bitterman's martyrdom, two hundred new volunteers came forward to serve in Bible translation. His death illustrates how God brings good out of evil (Genesis 50:15–21). The grain of wheat that falls to the earth and dies bears much fruit (John 12:24).

We gain courage by learning of Anglican Bishop Festo Kivengere of Uganda. Kivengere faced and accused the "wild man of Africa"—the mad dictator Idi Amin—of abusing his authority, warning him that he would be judged by God. Kivengere inspires us to stand boldly for the Lord, no matter what the opposition.

Floyd McClung and his family likewise provide an example that only the courageous can follow. In spite of the obvious dangers, Floyd and his wife, Sally, raised their family while working in urban ministry: first in Kabul, Afghanistan—reaching out to drug addicts and seekers on the "hippie trail"; and then in Amsterdam, Netherlands—living in an apartment building located between the Church of Satan and a house of prostitution. Their lives remind us that God works today even as he did for Daniel in the lions' den and for David before Goliath—to protect his faithful people.[9]

Dr. Brian Stiller, president of Tyndale University College and Seminary in Toronto, Canada, illustrated the dramatic impact of the saints who have gone before us by telling the story of a young American football player. This young man was, at best, an average player, spending most games sitting on the bench. Occasionally, the player would bring his father to the games, and it always struck the coach that the father seemed to hang on his son when they walked away after the game.

One day the coach got word that the young man's father had died. He went to pay his respects, and to his surprise, the young player made a request: "Coach," he said, "will you grant me one wish?"

The coach, cautious not to hurt the already grieved young man, said, "Well, sure, I'll try."

The young player responded, "Please let me start in the game tomorrow."

The coach did not know how to answer. He wanted to grant the grieving boy's request, but he knew it was an important game. Not wanting to go back on his word, however, he consented.

In the next game, the young man was sent in to play, with the coach thinking, *I'll pull him back on the bench as soon as he starts making mistakes.* To the coach's surprise, however, the young man played extraordinarily well. He was everywhere on the field, executing tackles, making big plays, and exceeding any performance the coach had ever seen before in practice.

After the game, the coach approached the young man and asked, "What got into you today? I never expected you to do so well, especially after your father's death."

"But, Coach," the young man responded, "I played that well because of my father's death. You see, Coach, my father was blind. So this was the first game he ever saw me play."

The thought of his father in that "great cloud of witnesses" motivated the young man to do his best. As we are inspired to action by the heroes of faith who have gone before us, we build our commitment to grow as world-class Christians on the second foundation stone—the inspiration of the saints.

Emotion Will Not Keep Us

The tragic story of Hank Gathers teaches us the power of emotion. When we confront the realities of eternity and the death of millions of people without Christ, our emotions will be stirred.

But an emotional response is limited. We cannot sustain our vision on emotion alone. Instead, we build our world-class vision, action, and commitment on the following facts:

- Almighty God, the Creator of the ends of the earth, reveals himself to be God of all people and nations, and he solicits our participation in bringing these people to understand his gospel and his glory.

- God reveals himself as the one true Savior (Isaiah 43:11), and his primary revelation is through his Son, Jesus Christ. There is salvation found in no one else (Acts 4:12), because he alone is the way, the truth, and the life by which all people must come to God (John 14:6). This unique Savior must be proclaimed to a world with no hope outside of him.
- We are not alone. A great cloud of witnesses has gone before us, and as we get to know their lives, we are motivated and encouraged to persevere ourselves.

Action Items

A solid world-class vision needs information. Here are four practical ways to build our information base about the Word of God and the inspiration of others:

1. Read a book that provides an overview of God's global mandate given throughout the Scriptures. John Piper's *Let the Nations Be Glad* and William Dyrness's *Let the Earth Rejoice!* are good places to start.

2. Look up in a Bible concordance (over a period of days or weeks) all the verses that contain the word "world," "earth," or "nations." You'll be amazed at how many there are.

3. Wrestle with the biblical teaching that Jesus Christ stands as the *only* Savior; therefore, all people without him are spiritually lost. This is a foundational conviction in the worldwide spread of Christianity. But, in our pluralistic culture—where we want to believe that everyone's beliefs are okay—we struggle to accept it. Study John 14:6 and 1 Timothy 2:4, and then consider these questions: How can people be saved without Jesus as their Savior? If some can be saved without knowing Jesus Christ, then why did

he need to come and die? Three helpful books on this issue are the following: Paul Borthwick, *Six Dangerous Questions to Transform Your View of the World;* J. Robertson McQuilkin, *The Great Omission;* and Don Richardson, *Eternity in Their Hearts.*

4. Read *From Jerusalem to Irian Jaya* by Ruth Tucker. This compendium represents probably the finest tool available for understanding the work of God through the saints over the ages. With succinct, two- to six-page sketches, the reader meets the most notable personalities of two thousand years of Christian mission. If you don't want to read the entire book, the illustration index of the book will direct you to saints whose lives illustrate topics such as Christ-centeredness, endurance, reconciliation, sacrifice, and success.

Biblical Texts to Study

- 2 Kings 5:1–19 (Elisha)

- Esther 3:7–4:17 (Esther)

- Daniel 6:4–28 (Daniel)

- Jonah 1:1–17; 3:1–4:11 (Jonah)

- Acts 8:4–8, 26–40 (Philip)

- Acts 16:11–40 (Paul)

Things to Talk About

- Referencing the Scriptures above, to whom did God send each person? Why?

- How did God use each person?

- What were the results of their ministries?

- What do we learn about God from these events?

- What do we learn from biblical and recent missionaries that can motivate us to grow and persevere as world-class believers?

4

INFORMATION AND ISSUES

A world-class Christian lifestyle is compatible with what God is doing in our world.

Anthropologists identify people from the earliest stages of society as "hunters and gatherers," those people who foraged through the fields and forests, gathering berries and roots and other edibles for their sustenance. I like to think of world-class Christians as "hunters and gatherers" of a different type. To further our growth, we are always hunting for information and gathering data about issues in the world into which God calls us. Building on the two-part foundation of the Scriptures and the saints, we continue to grow by foraging through websites, books, newspapers, and a host of other sources to expand our minds concerning God's great world.

Hunting for information and gathering data is a lifelong challenge, so let's consider some of the habits of world-class Christians.

Information

Do we live in a global village? While those who focus their lives on worldwide issues continue to discuss the miniaturization of our world, many of us, at least in the United States, seem to be increasingly ignorant about the world and its affairs. It's almost as if the rich get richer (that is, those whose jobs are global in nature continue to learn about intercultural issues, worldwide developments, and international economies) while the poor get poorer (that is, those who are not required to learn about world issues diminish in their knowledge of world events).

Brian O'Connell recalled an incident that occurred when he served with the National Association of Evangelicals in Washington, D.C. Sixteen candidates for a U.S. senatorial seat were given a "pop quiz" on current events. Out of five questions, only one candidate answered more than two questions correctly. O'Connell concluded: "Unfortunately, this lack of knowledge among leaders reflects a lack of information and concern for international affairs among the bulk of our society. Almost without exception, polls show that Americans are uninformed and unconcerned about international events."[1]

The problem of geographic ignorance expands beyond our political leaders. The National Geographic/Roper Public Affairs 2006 Geographic Literacy Study paints a dismal picture of the geographic knowledge of the most-recent graduates of the U.S. education system. They discovered that graduates between the ages of eighteen and twenty-four were woefully unaware of global matters:

- *fewer than three in ten* graduates think it important to know the locations of countries in the news, and just 14 percent believe that speaking another language is a necessary skill
- *66 percent* could not find Iraq or Saudi Arabia on a map; 75 percent could not point out Iran or Israel; *45 percent* couldn't find any one of those four countries
- *88 percent* of those questioned could not find Afghanistan on a map of Asia
- *47 percent* could not find the Indian subcontinent on a map of Asia

- *nearly three-quarters* incorrectly named English as the most widely spoken native language
- *six in ten* did not know that the border between North and South Korea is the most heavily fortified border in the world; *30 percent* thought the most heavily fortified border was between the United States and Mexico

The final report concluded, "Taken together, these results suggest that young people in the United States . . . are unprepared for an increasingly global future."[2]

Is this lack of knowledge also among Christians? Happily, I've found that an increased desire to know God's purposes in the world is leading many Christians to grow in their concern for world events. Pastors include global issues in their pastoral prayers. Churches rise up to care for refugees in their area. Cross-cultural workers find increased interest in global issues when they bring home reports of their work, and international Christian leaders find themselves issuing challenges from many North American pulpits.

But we still have many opportunities to grow!

Gather Global Information

Gathering global information can help us build a world-class Christian vision. Where to start? How about purchasing an up-to-date map? A global-outreach team at one church asked me what they could do to expand their church's world vision. I suggested they post a world map in a prominent place in the foyer. One member proudly responded, "We already have one." I went to see it.

The huge map covered the wall facing the sanctuary. Everyone would see it when they walked in. That was the good news. The bad news? On the map, country names such as the USSR were outdated; East and West Germany were divided; and Czechoslovakia and Yugoslavia were united. Anyone who knew the modern world would look at this map and think, *This church has a world vision, but they are considerably out-of-date.*

One school of business management, encouraging readers to "take global education seriously," wrote:

> American citizens may be among the world's most prosperous, but according to a recent *National Geographic* study conducted by the Gallup Poll, their geographical knowledge is hardly world-class, in the nine-nation survey of 10,820 adults, U.S. respondents finished third from the bottom. . . . Among the American respondents, 75 percent failed to locate the Persian Gulf on a map. At the same time, fewer than half could find the United Kingdom, France, South Africa, or Japan. Using blank maps, the average American could identify only four of twelve European nations, and fewer than six of ten U.S. states. Perhaps most humiliating, one in seven U.S. adults could not identify the United States on a map.[3]

Buy a map! Better yet, buy a copy of *Operation World* or visit operationworld.org. This collection of global-Christian knowledge outlines every country of the world for study over the course of 365 days. It also gives pertinent data and specific prayer requests for each country. *Operation World* (updated about every three years) provides an excellent source of global information while helping us with current geography.

Knowing the world in which we live is essential for functioning effectively as world-class Christians. Gilbert Grosvenor of *National Geographic* warns, "Our adult population, especially our young adults, do not understand the world at a time in our history when we face a critical economic need to understand foreign consumers, markets, customs, opportunities, and responsibilities."[4]

Grosvenor's concern is economic. Our concern goes beyond that, since God calls us to be his ambassadors (2 Corinthians 5:20). Ignorance of our world can discredit our witness. An international student from Peru told me of being introduced to an American who said, "Oh yes, Peru, the islands off the coast of Ecuador."

"No," the student politely replied. "You are thinking of the Galapagos Islands. Peru is the country directly below Ecuador."

"No, I think *you* are incorrect," the American replied belligerently, and the conversation came to an abrupt halt.

My Peruvian friend told me that the conversation was not ruined by the American's incorrect location of Peru—many international people are tolerant of our geographic ignorance. "It was his arrogance, telling me that I did not know where my own country is located." An opportunity to be an "ambassador of Christ" was lost because of arrogance added to geographic ignorance.

Read

Reading can further our informational growth. A myriad of rich opportunities are available to us through the printed media. Larry, the chair of his church's global-outreach committee, is a self-taught global specialist. By trade, he is an electrician, but a unique situation in his job grants him some time to read. His global information gathering, unsurpassed in his church, includes periodicals, biographies, books about mission strategy, and even sections of David Barrett's mammoth work, *The World Christian Encyclopedia*. Larry stands as an example to us that the information is out there—if we're willing to discipline ourselves to read.

For some, disciplined reading comes only in a structured learning situation. A course on international business, cross-cultural understanding, or even geography and history might serve as a catalyst for world-class learning. Perspectives on the World Christian Movement (a ministry of the U.S. Center for World Mission, uscwm.org), a course which provides an excellent overview of the movement, has stimulated thousands of Christian to become world-class in broadening their understanding of our world.

World-class information gathering can also include choosing an international news website as a homepage, reading the international section of the newspaper, catching excerpts of God's work around the world through publications from agencies that work in other cultures, or consulting global reports. Some choose a specific global issue about which they want to learn, so they receive, for example, updates about the church in China, prayer requests on behalf of the persecuted church, or reports on the challenges facing those working against human trafficking. The Google and Yahoo search engines can help us find amazing information quickly.

Observe News and Entertainment Media

Radio, the Internet, television, and movies can foster greater growth of our knowledge of the world. In one church, members of the global-outreach team have Skype accounts so they can communicate with their partners around the world. A man interested in radio ministry listens to radio station HCJB out of Quito, Ecuador, "simply to hear the gospel going out in another language." My wife and I listen to the "World News" broadcast of the BBC as well as reports on National Public Radio (NPR), because these offer more in-depth reporting on international events that may not be covered by network news stations.

Cable News Network (CNN) opens global horizons to us. Some grow by watching programs related to cultures, nature, or international events featured on the Public Broadcasting Service (PBS). *National Geographic* television specials take us around the world, educating us and giving us fuel to pray for people, cultures, and places we may never see firsthand.

One friend collects DVDs about other parts of the world. *Hotel Rwanda, Bend It Like Beckham,* and even *My Big Fat Greek Wedding* all have some value in educating us about culture and history. Documentaries can provide enjoyable ways for us to learn. The film *End of the Spear* offers us information and insight about forgiveness as well as educates us about the famous martyrdom in 1955 of five young men in Ecuador.

In all this learning, the goal is not merely cognitive growth. Instead, we seek information so that we might be effective ambassadors of Christ in the immediate world into which he sends us. After hearing of a courageous Cambodian man who returned to Cambodia to find and forgive the man who had killed a dozen of his family members during the genocide led by the Khmer Rouge, I realized afresh the power of the gospel to enable people to forgive. A businessman, after hearing of the spread of the gospel in China—in spite of opposition—wrote, "A report like that makes it easy for guys like me to go out into the marketplace during the week with motivation to present the gospel with excitement."

Observe Modern Mission Trends

What do cross-cultural workers actually do? This question further stirs our quest for knowledge of God's work in the world. But many of us need answers that are more contemporary—past images of white, pith-helmeted missionaries carrying the gospel to helpless savages desperately need updating. Cross-cultural workers now come from every continent and go to every continent. The countries from which the new cross-cultural workers come include South Korea, Nigeria, Brazil, and India. Countries that were formerly the receivers of missionaries are now sending them—often back to the Western sending countries. Did you know that a Nigerian missionary is the pastor of perhaps the largest Protestant church in Europe (in Kiev, Ukraine)?

Learning about God's people serving in other countries teaches us that not every cross-cultural worker establishes new churches. Some, working with relief and development ministries, plant trees. "Tentmakers" use their business, teaching, medical, political, or engineering skills to gain access to countries that do not allow traditional missionaries. Some international ambassadors of Christ go as pioneers to primitive tribes, working in inaccessible jungles;

but now many others go as pioneers to modern cities, working in urban jungles.

World-class information gathering means enlarging our vision of what is being done—and what remains to be done—by the international network of Christian workers in a variety of contexts and cultures.

Make Missions Fun

One last word about information gathering: Make it fun! Learning about cultures might include an international meal. And studying the map does not require sitting in the library; instead, buy a world-map beach ball, and study it while getting a tan. My friend Larry does an enormous amount of reading, including reading children's books—from picture books to coloring books to easy-to-read biographies such as Sheila Miller's *My Book about Hudson* (Hudson Taylor, missionary to China).

Expand your world knowledge and have some geographic fun by deciphering twelve capitals of Europe from these anagrams:[5]

1. LOBS IN	7. LEG BEARD
2. DID ARM	8. WAS RAW
3. SHIN-LIKE	9. CUB'S HEART
4. I SPAR	10. OPEN CHANGE
5. A TRAIN	11. HAS TEN
6. GEAR UP	12. NON-OLD

Issues

Hunting for international information coincides with gathering data pertaining to issues that threaten the spread of the gospel. While there are hundreds of issues to focus upon, there are several mega-issues of which we should at least be aware (and perhaps every church should give at least partial consideration to the following mega-issues during the course of the year).

Morris Watkins identified some of these mega-issues back in the 1980s, but his book *Seven Worlds to Win* is still amazingly relevant today.[6] Watkins identified the following greatest challenges facing the spread of worldwide Christianity:

1. The Chinese world (one of every five people on earth)
2. The Hindu world (and the "New Age" carryover into the Western world)
3. The Buddhist world (much of South Asia)
4. The Muslim world (with a zeal to do its own brand of "evangelizing")
5. The Communist world (the USSR might be gone, but China, Vietnam, Cuba, and North Korea remain under this umbrella, and some predict that countries in the former USSR may return to communism)
6. The Bibleless/illiterate world (many languages still have no translation of the Bible, and some countries still have staggeringly high illiteracy rates)
7. The so-called Christian world (where Christianity is traditional, but not personal)

In the class that I teach at Gordon College on issues facing global Christianity, I often use Watkins's "mega-issues" as a springboard, but I expand the issues to further include the following:

- *The victims of disease and disaster.* HIV/AIDS and malaria kill millions of people annually. And chronic needs created by earthquakes, floods, tsunamis, and pollution contribute to human suffering.
- *The poor, the needy, and the hungry.* One billion people suffer each day from hunger, many barely surviving in one of the thousands of slum neighborhoods around the world. There are now 1 million street people in Calcutta.

- *Urbanization.* By the year 2010, an estimated 75 percent of the world's population will live in an urban center. There are currently over three hundred world-class cities, cities with populations exceeding 1 million. I live in the six-state region called New England, which has a population of about 14 million people. Contrast this with Shanghai (China), Mexico City, Manila (the Philippines), Cairo (Egypt), or Delhi (India). *Each* of these cities has a population that exceeds my entire region—and in fewer square miles. Imagine the challenges!

- *Youth and children.* Over 35 percent of the people in the majority world are under age fifteen, and 50 percent are under age twenty-five. And many of these are growing up in poverty.

- *The environment.* This mega-issue ought to concern us all. No matter where we fall on the spectrum of assigning blame or predicting disaster, we can agree that the environment is being affected by human pollution.

Although lists like these oversimplify our world, they do assist us in grasping the major issues facing the church around the world. Any one of these issues—or others we may want to pursue, such as the growing non-Western missionary movement cited earlier, or the work needed to empower the poor, or the need for a Christian transformational impact in the city—can occupy us for the next decade. But a little information about each issue and specific information on one issue can help us to be acutely aware of the challenges to come.

Implementation

How do we find information and gather data on issues? Any reasonable person could discount the suggestions given in this chapter as unreasonable in light of the vast amount of information available.

But instead of being overwhelmed, why not get started? Choose an issue, a country, a hot topic, or a people group, and dive in:

1. Ask God to give you opportunities to learn about your study topic. Several of our students started praying for Burkina Faso, West Africa. Suddenly they started noticing articles on the Web, seeing TV programs, and meeting people related to that tiny country. As they prayed, God opened new horizons of opportunity to learn.

2. Save articles found on the Internet and in newspapers and news magazines, creating your own information file. I never realized how much was written on Mozambique until several years ago, when preparing for a trip there, I started a file. Now it bulges with articles that help me understand and pray for the church in that country.

3. Search on the Google or Yahoo search engine for recent books and articles on your topic. With so many events changing in our world, there is often too much information to choose from, especially if the study topic is a "hot spot" that's often in the news.

4. Utilize cross-cultural friends. Building cross-cultural friendships—through an outreach to international students, through short-term mission relationship building, or even through an online tool like Facebook—can provide a firsthand report on something we're watching on the news. A text message, an email, or a call with our global network of friends can make international events come alive, providing us with firsthand reports and prayer requests that will be greater and more personal than any news broadcast.

5. Attend a seminar or lecture on your topic. Bill, a friend interested in China and especially Tibet, recently attended a lecture at a nearby college given by two scholars from Lhasa, Tibet's capital. Cultural lectures at museums, libraries, or colleges are often free of charge and provide excellent opportunities to ask questions.

6. Pool your information. A group studying massive issues like AIDS in Africa or hunger in Asia will accumulate much more information than any one individual could—and the group learning can be stimulating and fun.

See What God Is Doing

If we want to become world-class Christians, we need to develop a *bifocal* vision. Remember bifocals, the glasses that had two sections, one to correct nearsightedness and the other to correct farsightedness? We need a bifocal global vision:

nearsighted vision: looking close at hand to the needs around us, and

farsighted vision: looking beyond ourselves to the world of need and opportunity outside of our normal sphere of influence.

Finding information and gathering data about global issues can add perspective to our understanding of the world into which God calls us and add power to our prayers for the world. As we forage through the stories of God at work in the world, we sing the following words with Scott Wesley Brown:

Look what God is doing
All across the land,
See his Spirit moving
Feel his mighty hand.

Breaking chains of darkness,
Setting captives free;
Look what God is doing
Through those who do believe.

Glory Halleluiah, look what God is doing,
He is calling faithful men
To carry out his plan.
So in the power of Jesus' name
Go possess the land.

Take the living Gospel,
Mix it with some love,
Add a little action,
And see what our God does.
Glory Halleluiah, look what God is doing![7]

Biblical Texts to Study

- Matthew 9:36–38

- Matthew 28:18–20

- Acts 1:6–8

Things to Talk About

- What do we see God doing in our world today, and where?

• Referencing the Scriptures above, what does God want to "do" in our world through us?

• How do God's ways of "doing" mission compare with our ways?

• What is your specific area of mission interest (such as a country, a people group, a cross-cultural worker, or an issue)? How is God working in that area?

• What major issues challenge the spread of the gospel in our world today?

• Identify ways you can increase your "bifocal" knowledge of God's world and his work in it.

A LOOK AT WORLD-CLASS PRAYERS

The saint who advances on his knees never retreats.

JIM ELLIOT

Our team of fourteen arrived at Moffat College of Bible in Kijabe, Kenya, almost two days after we left home. We were safe and mostly rested, having endured two all-night flights, an all-day layover, two customs checks, cramped seats, and a variety of airplane food.

In contrast to other work teams that Christie and I had led, traveling with this one seemed almost too easy. The details, transfers, visa checkpoints, and a myriad of other loose ends that make up such a trip were flawlessly accomplished. In Nairobi, twenty-two pieces of luggage rolled off the belt unscathed, a miracle on any connecting flight.

When we introduced ourselves to the students at Moffat College, a student leader welcomed us: "For four months we have been praying for you every day, and now you are here. *Karibu*" ("welcome" in Swahili).

In those words, we realized that our flawless travel was not due to our leadership or planning. We were on the receiving end of faithful, consistent prayer. We benefited because brothers and sisters who had never met us were faithful in prayer on our behalf. Our lives, travel, and safety had been touched, protected, and guided by our God in response to the prayers of people we did not know.

If we had any lofty thoughts of teaching spiritual disciplines to these African brothers and sisters from Kenya, Uganda, Tanzania, Chad, and Sudan, they dissipated in this welcome. The students at Moffat College of Bible humbled us. We felt convicted by our own failure to pray. But we also realized that God had worked through their prayers, and in them, we saw the importance of prayer on a global scale. Because of the world-class nature of their prayers, our world was changed. Through them, we realized that prayer is our greatest asset for being a partner in God's work around the world. God wants to change the world, and he will do it through our prayers and through us.

Biblical World-Class Prayers

The Bible introduces us to a host of men and women who led the way in offering world-class prayers. None (except Jesus) were perfect, and several (David and Solomon) are known as much for their sins as for their sanctification. Nonetheless, their prayers—preserved for us by God forever in the Scriptures—give us a glimpse of the worship of God that extends far beyond cultural and geographic biases.

Miriam

Consider Miriam, Moses' sister. Her prayer of worship and praise is offered after the escape of the Israelites through the Red Sea. Miriam leads the people of Israel in a song to the Lord, as recorded in Exodus 15:20–21.

Her prayer focuses on God's victory. *The Lord* wins the battle. *The Lord* throws the enemies into the sea. *The Lord* defeats the greatest army in the world. *The Lord* uses his power to overrule nature and achieve his purposes. All his enemies will fear because the God of Israel is the one true God. *The Lord* will reign forever and ever.

Miriam's prayer is world-class because she points us to one of the greatest global themes in the Bible—God will win the victory. His kingdom will be established. He will defeat those who boast against him, and he will lead his people into the final winner's circle, the message of the Book of Revelation.

Lucy exemplifies prayer in the spirit of Miriam. This faithful prayer champion attacks the most difficult issues of the day in her prayers. In the past, her prayer focus was the nation of Albania, a country whose dictator boasted until the 1980s that his was "the only truly atheist nation on earth." Now she targets her prayers on places like North Korea, the most radical Muslim nations, and war-torn areas like Sudan and Sri Lanka. When Lucy prays, she prays with fervor but not panic, with zeal but not anxiety, with seriousness but not worry. She knows that God will win the final victory, that the powers now opposing the gospel will fall just as Pharaoh's army was swallowed up in the Red Sea. She knows that she is on the winning team.

World-class prayer principle 1: God is the victor, the ultimate Lord of history. When we approach the topic of prayer for our world, we need to know that God is the winner. He is not worried. He will lead the church to final triumph, a triumph started in Jesus' death on the cross and completed in his return (see Matthew 16:18).

Hannah

Hannah exemplifies another world-class prayer. After she prayed long and hard for a child, God answered her prayer by giving her a son, Samuel. Hannah dedicates Samuel to God with her prayer recorded in 1 Samuel 2:1–10. Even though Hannah lacked any type of formal education, her prayer is remarkably articulate about the character of God as the Sovereign Judge of the earth:

> The LORD brings death, and makes alive;
> he brings down to the grave and raises up.
> The LORD sends poverty and wealth;
> he humbles and he exalts.
> He raises the poor from the dust
> and lifts the needy from the ash heap;
> he seats them with princes
> and has them inherit a throne of honor. . . .
> The LORD will judge the ends of the earth.
> (1 Samuel 2:6–8, 10)

Hannah's prayer brings great hope to any who suffer under the clutches of oppression. To us in wealthier nations, however, her prayer rebukes any self-satisfaction or self-reliance we might feel. We dare not enter into the world advancement of the church thinking that our wealth and success are somehow a result of our own doing. We are what we are because God has allowed it. Knowing the Sovereign Judge, who exalts one and puts down another, squelches our feelings of superiority toward any other people on earth.

Also, Hannah's prayer foreshadows the experience of King Nebuchadnezzar. In his power, opulence, and success, he deceives himself into thinking that he is self-sufficient: "Is this not the great Babylon I have built as the royal residence, by *my* mighty power and for the glory of *my* majesty?" (Daniel 4:30, emphasis mine). At such arrogance, God strikes the king down, reducing him to an animal-like madman. Only when King Nebuchadnezzar comes to his senses and submits himself before God is he restored:

Then I praised the Most High; I honored and glorified him who lives forever.

> His dominion is an eternal dominion;
> his kingdom endures from generation to generation.
> All the peoples of the earth
> are regarded as nothing.
> He does as he pleases
> with the powers of heaven
> and the peoples of the earth.
> No one can hold back his hand
> or say to him, "What have you done?"
> (Daniel 4:34–35)

Nebuchadnezzar concludes, "And those who walk in pride he is able to humble" (Daniel 4:37).

World-class prayer principle 2: God is the Sovereign Judge; all that we have and are comes from his goodness and mercy. Nebuchadnezzar and Hannah remind any who possess power and wealth that these gifts are given by the Sovereign Judge and must be used to his glory!

King David and King Solomon

King David's prayers appear throughout the Old Testament, especially in the Psalms. His final prayer, however, is recorded in 2 Samuel 22:2–51, just before his death. David's prayer focuses on deliverance, on worshiping God because of his creative greatness, and on God's faithfulness.

In the midst of this great prayer—just as he completes a hymn on God's awesome power in creation (vv. 8–16)—David records one of the most profound personal truths in the Bible. "He reached down from on high and took hold of me" (v. 17). The Almighty God, the Creator of the ends of the earth, took hold of me!

David points us to the great and awesome King of the Universe who takes an interest *in us*. He also reminds us that, in some mysterious way, the Sovereign Lord of all has divinely limited himself to work *through us*.

World-class prayer principle 3: God is personal; he who rules the universe desires relationship with us. Of all the truths that thrust us forward into God's worldwide action, this truth is perhaps the greatest: *God wants to use our lives!* In the midst of worship, we realize that God has reached down to take hold of us through Jesus. When we understand this, we cannot help but join David in committing ourselves to praise him among the nations (v. 50).

King Solomon, most famous for his wisdom and his temple, utilized both to offer an extraordinary prayer of dedication in 1 Kings 8:22–61. Realizing that God is not limited to this physical structure (v. 27), Solomon still prays that his temple will be a place where God hears . . .

. . . to forgive

. . . to judge

. . . to save the foreigner.

In a world where most of Solomon's subjects were satisfied to hold the God of Israel as uniquely theirs, Solomon expands their vision through his prayer. He dedicates the temple that it may serve foreigners (non-Israelites), "so that *all the peoples of the earth* may know your name and fear you" (v. 43, emphasis mine) and "so that *all the peoples of the earth* may know that the LORD is God and there is no other" (v. 60, emphasis mine).

World-class prayer principle 4: God hears and forgives so that his glory might be known in all the earth. In our world, where the Christian church is often content to build structures and programs that serve only the saved, we are wise to listen to Solomon. All that we do should be done to foster true worship of the Lord Most High—so that all the peoples of the world may know him.

Daniel

Daniel is our final Old Testament example. A true missionary in a pagan culture, Daniel faced a world that challenged his morals, his spirituality, and his convictions. Yet he endured under the reigns of four kings as a wise and faithful voice for the Lord. One of his prayers illustrates at least one of the secrets of his staying power. Facing a baffling dream that no one could interpret, Daniel approaches the Lord for discernment of the dream. In Daniel 2:20–23, Daniel worships God as the giver of discernment, wisdom, power, and knowledge.

In a similar way, the mother of Hudson Taylor relied on God for discernment. While struggling with frustration over the unconverted state of her teenage son, she, like modern parents, knew of no solution. She devoted herself to prayer, and over a two-week time of separation from her family, she sensed the Lord leading her to pray faithfully for his salvation. She prayed until she was certain God had answered her prayer.

When she returned home, her son reported to her of his personal conversion after reading gospel tracts. God, the giver of discernment, led Mrs. Taylor to pray, while he worked in the heart of her young son, who would become the greatest missionary pioneer of the nineteenth century.

Both Daniel and Mrs. Taylor illustrate a resolve to pray over issues that concern us. In our time, when we convince ourselves that we must spend our energies figuring things out and taking action, perhaps we would do better if we first went to God and asked for discernment.

World-class prayer principle 5: God gives discernment; he opens our minds to understand the times in which we live so that we can respond wisely. As we approach a world that baffles us, Daniel gives us a clue as to the priority of praying for discernment. Acknowledging that our time in history is too troubling for us to understand, we can come confidently before God, asking him to reveal the "deep and hidden things."

Jesus

Jesus, in the New Testament, instructs us to pray, "Your kingdom come, your will be done on earth as it is in heaven" (Matthew 6:10). His priority in prayer is that God's will be done on earth.

This priority resulted in Jesus' call to die. When facing his final betrayal into the hands of his enemies, Jesus offers his greatest prayer (John 17). In spite of the personal suffering that lay ahead for him, Jesus prays for his disciples and all who would come after them (including us). His prayer focuses directly on God's kingdom being declared on earth. He prays that Christians will be unified in order "to let the world know that you sent me and have loved them even as you have loved me" (John 17:23).

In other words, Jesus prays not for his own safety or success. Instead, he prays for the unity of Christians so that the world might know the gospel. He demonstrates to us that our prayers should not be anchored to our personal concerns, but they should go beyond these to the spread of the gospel. Even when it involves personal discomfort, the coming of the kingdom through the united body of Christ is our highest concern.

Mrs. Josephine Kennedy began praying in the late 1940s for God to raise up a witness to himself in the northwestern suburbs of

Boston. She cared only for Christ to be exalted, and for several years, she alone carried this ministry of prayer.

By the early fifties, others joined her in prayer, believing that God wanted to raise up a church in their community of Lexington. They formed a fellowship group, and in faith, they laid aside some denominational nuances to form an interdenominational church. Steps of faith, prayer, and an outward focus on witness and missions prevailed.

Over sixty years later, Mrs. Kennedy's prayers continue to be answered. The church that God raised up in answer to her prayers has grown to over two thousand members, with significant local and global outreaches. Over $1 million is given annually to support the cross-cultural workers and international partners working in more than thirty countries. One hundred or more youth and adults participate in cross-cultural mission teams, and there is an ongoing active witness in the local community and the Boston area. Following her spirit and the spirit of Christ in John 17, Grace Chapel (grace.org) still chooses not to be divided over issues that often divide churches (eschatology, the charismatic movement, and so on), but to unite around the centrality of declaring Christ to the world.

World-class prayer principle 6: Jesus' kingdom and the united action of believers should take precedence over our own personal issues. Will we pray for the spread of the gospel in our area, even if God answers our prayers by granting growth to the church down the street? Will we go beyond our own needs and pray for those whose needs make ours look insignificant? Will we pray for other Christian groups to be successful, even though we may disagree with some of their doctrinal positions? For the body of Christ, God's will done on earth is our highest prayer, accompanied by our united actions that demonstrate to others his love.

Paul

The apostle Paul offers one more example of world-class prayer. In Ephesians 1:15–23 and then in the great benediction of Ephesians 3:20–21, Paul lifts our eyes upward to see the greatness of God. Hope in him motivates us to carry on, and the great assignment of declaring his glory is made possible because of his power.

When we come to the challenge of world evangelization with the realization that Jesus is the beginning and the end of what we do, we cannot help but join Paul in worshiping him who is able to do "immeasurably more than all we ask or imagine" (Ephesians 3:20).

In the late 1940s and the early 1950s, God called many to pray Ephesians 1:15–23 prayers for the estimated 1 million Chinese Christians who were left without missionaries or foreign helpers after Mao Tse-tung came to power. The People's Republic of China stands today as a testimony of God changing the world through prayer. Those missionaries who were ousted by Mao "left China on their knees and never got up. They left physically but never spiritually."[2] Carl Lawrence pays tribute to these people of world-changing prayer:

> They were not defeated; they simply continued to do battle in one of the toughest arenas of all: intercessory prayer. They were often maligned for not realizing that this was a "different world we live in, and there is nothing you can do for China." Few were (or have been) recognized for their contribution to the building of his kingdom. They nevertheless continued hour by hour, day by day, and year by year, remembering by name those they left behind in the villages and communities that spread across China. Their work was far beyond any job description which man might design.[3]

Without exaggeration, those who committed themselves to pray for China experienced "more than [they could] ask or imagine" when the doors to China began to reopen in the 1970s. Reports came out that the Christian church of 1 million had grown to over 50 million. Today, conservative estimates put the evangelical church at 100 million. China is a remarkable testimony to the power of the Holy Spirit to bring "glory in the church and in Christ Jesus throughout all generations, forever and ever" (Ephesians 3:21).

> World-class prayer principle 7: Expectation. When we pray for ourselves and for other believers around the world, we do so with the anticipation that God will act mightily so that all may "know the hope to which he has called you, the riches of his glorious inheritance in the saints, and his incomparably great power for us who believe" (Ephesians 1:18-19).

Other saints in the Scriptures also offer prayers that instruct us about praying with an enlarged worldview. The world-class prayers described in this chapter are just a few select examples. They teach us not only how to grow in prayer but also that God is the starting point of prayer. Their example of prayer shows that a majority of their attention focused on some aspect of the character of God, and from that vantage point of worship, their view of the world was changed. The same will happen for us when we focus on who God is and allow our prayers to flow from this vision.

Why Prayer?

All of us would like to be part of changing the world, but prayer seems so docile. Why not dedicate ourselves to action? Why spend time cultivating and building the discipline of prayer?

The Task Is Too Big for Us

If accumulating world information does not overwhelm us, the needs of people certainly will. Some of us will be overcome by emotion while others retreat because of an acute sense of guilt. All of these reactions lead to one basic conclusion: We cannot accomplish God's purposes in our own strength.

When Jesus saw the crowds as "harassed and helpless, like sheep without a shepherd" (Matthew 9:36), he did not command his disciples to run around in frenzied activity, trying to meet all the needs. He commanded them to pray (Matthew 9:38) that the Lord of the harvest would act.

We pray, staying focused on the fact that Jesus is the Lord of this harvest. Harassed and helpless people will overwhelm us if we are not hearing first from the Commander who sends us out. Tom Wells explains the priority of prayer: "Prayer is our first work in the harvest. And the reason is not hard to find. It is this: the harvest has a 'Lord,' he oversees the harvest. Someone supplies the workers. Someone controls the progress. And that 'Someone' is God. *Our first business is not to look at the size of the harvest. Our first business is to pray to our God*"[4] (emphasis mine).

God Uses Prayer to Mold Us

Sometimes we come to prayer in an effort to change God's mind. By contrast, the biblical concept of prayer includes waiting on God so that he can change our will into his. God used three days in the belly of a fish to change Jonah's mind about obeying him and about going to Nineveh. In Jonah's time of prayer (What else could he do?), God molded Jonah's will into his own.

As we pray, God will change our thoughts, dreams, plans, and prayers. People now serving in cross-cultural situations often begin their stories by saying, "When I first became a Christian, the last thought in my mind was becoming a missionary." But in time, through their growth and prayer, God changed their minds. He used prayer to change their priorities, to reorient their values, and to alter their plans.

A friend who works in inner-city ministry told me of the effect prayer had in his life. He grew up in a church where subtle racism pervaded the cross-cultural outreach emphasis. Jokes about people being poor "because they were lazy" were common. The insinuation that nonwhites were somehow inherently inferior to whites affected his perspective as a young Christian. He finally sensed God calling him to cross-cultural ministry, and with a genuine desire to help "these poor black folks," he started to prepare. His preparation included prayer.

As my friend prayed, God began to change him. He read in the Scriptures about Samaritans and Gentiles and widows and the poor. He began to realize that the attitudes he had grown up with were sinful and destructive to the personal worth of those he was going to serve. The Holy Spirit convicted him of his racism, identified his pride, and gave him grace to repent. When he finally went to the inner city, his spirit had been transformed so that he could go as a servant, not a condescending leader.

When Jesus commands us to pray for our enemies, perhaps he uses our submission to him in prayer as one way to change our attitudes. When we open ourselves before God in prayer, he can do a ministry of the Spirit to change hate into love, racial stereotypes into sacrificial service, and bitterness into blessing.

Prayer Engages Us in Spiritual Warfare

James (Jim) Reapsome, former editor of the *Evangelical Missions Quarterly*, once published a study of global-outreach plans to spread the gospel. In this study, he noted the obstacles that could hinder the accomplishment of the Great Commission. Sadly, the first obstacle he cited is the church itself. Within the church, the first problem he detected is "prayerlessness."

Reapsome writes, "Global praying tends to be both too general and superficial, rather than specific and thorough." He went on to address the issue of spiritual warfare: "How can the barriers of Islam, Marxism, Hinduism, and Buddhism be broken down without pre-vailing, persistent prayer?"[5]

The Bible states that "we are not contending against flesh and blood, but against the principalities, against the powers, against the world rulers of this present darkness, against the spiritual hosts of wickedness in the heavenly places" (Ephesians 6:12 RSV). How can we hope to be world-changers without prayer?

Be a World-Changer: Pray

The news media like to catch our attention by publishing "factoids." Factoids might appear on your television screen just before a commercial break. They might be in a magazine or newspaper sidebar. They might pop up on a website. I clipped a factoid from *Reader's Digest* that caught my eye: "Pounds of plutonium and highly enriched uranium that are unaccounted for in U.S. inventories: 9,600. Pounds of plutonium needed to make an atomic bomb: 15."[6]

The point? A vast (and dangerous) amount of atomic bomb energy is unaccounted for. Thousands of pounds of plutonium are out there. Let's hope no one figures out how to tap that power for evil purposes.

That factoid made me think of the positive power available to us in prayer. A column in the *Heavenly Digest* might read: "Power to affect the world available through prayer: unlimited. World-class prayers being tapped: 15." God has given us access to his throne through prayer; he gives us the privilege to ask him to do beyond anything we can ask or think. But only a few Christians tap into his power.

Through our worship and intercession, we engage the Lord of the harvest. By our petitions, we can be part of his work around the world. Wesley Duewel, author of *Touch the World through Prayer*, suggests four ways that prayer involves us strategically in God's work around the world.[7] His insights still stand today.

1. Through prayer, we can join any team that God is using. We can join in the efforts of missionaries in the Amazon River valley, in the ministries of pastors in Sri Lanka, or in the evangelistic efforts of "tentmakers" in North Africa!

2. Our prayers can water the harvest. Literature distribution or radio broadcasts can sow the seed of the gospel, but we need to water this seed through our prayers.

3. Our prayers can cultivate the harvest. Many who do convert to Christ do so at the risk of their lives; we can be partners with these new believers—even as those were who prayed for Chinese Christians after 1950—through intercession on their behalf.

4. Our prayers can influence world leaders and change governments. We can pray that God uses world leaders to foster the spread of the gospel.

Dr. J. Christy Wilson was a world-changer through prayer. As a pastor in Afghanistan, he directly confronted the spiritual warfare of Islam. As professor of missions and dean of the Chapel at Gordon-Conwell Theological Seminary, Dr. Wilson played a part in God's worldwide ministry through his prayers. He has had a powerful impact on the lives of countless students (myself included!) because of his intercession on their behalf. His perseverance in prayer—praying regularly, by name, for each member of the student body and for the family of each student—has indelibly imprinted students who have graduated to go into ministries around the world.

What an opportunity we have to go to God in prayer and to beseech him—not only that he will make us like his Son but also that he will work mightily in the world! God invites us to be part of changing the world through prayer . . . how will you respond?

Biblical Texts to Study

- Exodus 15:1–18 (Moses)

- 1 Samuel 2:1–10 (Hannah)

- 1 Kings 8:22–34, 41–43, 56–61 (Solomon)

- Daniel 4:28–37 (Nebuchadnezzar)

- John 17:13–26 (Jesus)

- Ephesians 1:15–23; 3:14–21 (Paul)

Things to Talk About

• Referencing the Scriptures above, what elements do these world-class prayers have in common?

• What truths do we learn from these prayers about God and his view of the world?

- How do these biblical prayers compare with ours?

- If God is sovereign—in control of everything that happens—why should we bother to pray?

- How can we apply these truths about God and prayer to our areas of mission interest?

OUR PRAYERS CAN BE WORLD-CLASS

Satan laughs at our toiling, mocks our wisdom, but trembles
when we pray.

AN UNKNOWN CHRISTIAN, *THE KNEELING CHRISTIAN*

Christie and I sat with an American couple serving cross-culturally in Mozambique, a country in southeast Africa. Our church supported this couple, who served the national church in this war-ravaged, poverty-stricken country. We were visiting just after Mozambique had emerged from more than twenty years of civil war, and we listened to their difficulties with distributing food and clothing to people in desperate need. They sadly described the agony of thousands of people living on the edge of survival.

As they talked, a wave of helplessness overcame us. What could we possibly do? I asked the relief workers, "After we return home, is there anything we can do for you?"

They responded immediately. "Tell the people back home that *we are depending on their prayers!* We need God's supernatural help to continue this work." Then they quoted from 2 Corinthians. Paul the apostle wrote to the Corinthians as he and his team faced great persecution and hardship. He wrote of his hope in God's provision but appealed to the Corinthians for their partnership by stating, "On him [God] we have set our hope that he will continue to deliver us, *as you help us by your prayers*" (2 Corinthians 1:10–11, emphasis mine).

We can join God's worldwide team—helping others by our prayers—in the endeavor of communicating the gospel of Jesus Christ through word and deed.

We all have the incredible opportunity of participating in God's work worldwide, so why don't we? Let's consider three of the largest obstacles to prayer and some ideas on how to respond to them.

Obstacles to Prayer and our Responses

Obstacle 1: "It's too overwhelming."
Response: Pray manageably.

All of us can be overtaken by a similar wave of helplessness, such as the one we felt in Mozambique. But we cannot succumb to the temptation to quit. The answer lies in manageable praying. I cannot pray for millions of hurting children in our world; for example, I have difficulty focusing on Kenya, a country where 60 percent of the population is under age fourteen. But I can pray consistently for the Kenyan boy we support through World Vision. Using updates and reminders I receive from World Vision, I can participate in a ministry to this young man through prayer. By concentrating on one child, I can manage my response in prayer.

When I asked a man who was returning home for a year after serving in East Asia for five years the greatest way we, as a sending church, could encourage him, he responded immediately: "If one person in the church approached me and said, 'I have been praying for you *every* day,' I think I would start walking on air!" This man asked only that one person make it his or her manageable task to pray for him.

We can likewise pray manageably about world events. When the news outlets report a devastating earthquake, typhoon, or other natural disaster, manageable praying means lofting a "prayer arrow" (discussed in detail later in this chapter)—a brief prayer that we breathe to God about the crisis. We might pray for government leaders, relief coordinators, or local church leaders—asking God to guide their efforts in responding. Through a brief and manageable prayer, we can be involved in that event.

Obstacle 2: "But what do I pray about?"
Response: Pray practically.

We err when we think that prayer is limited to eloquent oratory in church-sounding English, using overused words such as "blessing" or "abundant" or even "thee" and "thou." We worship the Lord who taught us to pray for our daily bread. He welcomes our practical requests.

When we pray for others around the world, we often lack specifics. So we need to use our imaginations. I've started praying in an "ever-widening circle." That is, I start with that which I know and then move outward, letting God direct my prayers.

I might start by praying for Nicolas and Elizabeth Wafula in Kampala, Uganda. Nicolas directs a leadership development ministry; Elizabeth is a schoolteacher. I know the Wafulas, their family, and their co-workers, so I begin by praying for needs I am aware of. Then I move outward. I might pray (as God guides my imagination) that

- they will have success that day in meetings with government officials;
- God will keep them safe as they travel to leadership trainings in northern Uganda and into Sudan;
- they will make progress on the leadership center they are developing.

But then my circle widens. Remembering Nicolas and Elizabeth stirs me to pray for leaders at Uganda Christian University, for people there in student ministry through a group called Focus, and for Christian humanitarian workers responding to the needs of people suffering because of HIV/AIDS.

Praying in these ever-widening circles can lead us to pray by God's direction for needs that we otherwise might never know about.

Obstacle 3: "But will it make any difference?"
Response: Pray strategically.

Our prayers do make a difference. God promises to work through them, and many people—such as our friends in Mozambique—depend on the prayers of others.

To ensure the maximum effectiveness in our prayers, we pray strategically. As the Bible commands, we pray first for "kings and all those in authority" (1 Timothy 2:2), because these leaders hold the keys to the work of the gospel going forth. We might pray for government leaders to accelerate the efforts of a development project. Or we could ask God to work even through communist leaders to open the way for organizations such as the English Language Institute to bring the gospel through teachers into countries such as North Korea.

Strategic praying also calls us to pray for Christian leaders who guide the efforts of Christian work in their nations, such as Dr. George Chavanikamannil in north India, Emerson Boyce in Barbados, Ajith Fernando in Sri Lanka, and David Ruiz in Guatemala. If you would like to pray for specific Christian leaders around the world, the World Evangelical Alliance (worldevangelicals.org), Partners International (partnersintl.org), and the Lausanne Congress on World Evangelization (lausanne.org) are helpful places to find suggestions.

Join God's Worldwide Team: Pray

Paul wrote about Epaphras in his letter to the Colossians. Epaphras distinguished himself by "always wrestling in prayer" for the Colossian believers (Colossians 4:12).

We can be like Epaphras, wrestling in prayer for people we may never meet or for needs to which we cannot personally respond. Through prayer, we have the privilege and opportunity to touch our world.

David Howard, former general director of the World Evangelical Alliance, shared about world-class praying in his book *The Great Commission for Today*. In their younger years, Dave and Phyllis Howard were missionaries in Colombia, South America, where God seemed to be answering many prayers. There were many new believers, and God was mightily at work.

At the same time, Dave's older brother Phil toiled among the Slavey Indians in Canada's Northwest Territories. Phil had worked with these Indians for fourteen years—without one convert.

In a prayer meeting with the Indians in his village, Dave shared his concern for his brother Phil. The village leader rose and invited the people to pray. Dave described what happened: "He didn't have to repeat the invitation. Two hundred people went to their knees immediately and began to pray. Their custom is for all to pray out loud together. . . . That evening they prayed for one hour and fifteen minutes without stopping. They poured out their hearts for Phil, his wife Margaret, and for those Slavey Indians."[1]

The Colombian Indians' concern for Phil continued long after that prayer session. They sent letters to encourage him and persevered in prayer. David Howard later learned that Phil, after fourteen years of seemingly fruitless ministry, had reached an all-time low. He thought, *What's the use?* and wondered why he should continue. One night he went to bed defeated and discouraged; the next day he awoke with a new joy and courage to continue the work to which God had called him.

When the brothers compared dates, the times coincided exactly! The very night that Phil went to bed ready to quit and awoke revived was the night that those Colombian Indians spent time in zealous prayer on his behalf.

We can wrestle in prayer as part of our partnership in the worldwide body of Christ. Whether we pray regularly for a development project in Bangladesh, or for one child in Kenya, or for evangelistic efforts in Uzbekistan, we are essential parts of God's team.

Building Our Global Praying: 10 Steps to Get Started

Step 1: Start Where We Are and Build

If you've never prayed for anyone serving in another place, or for the church in other countries, or for leaders in foreign governments, let's get started![2] But don't overwhelm yourself by adding 168 countries or thirty-five missionaries to your prayers all at once. If we're praying for no one in another land now, we can start by praying for one person. As praying becomes an established discipline, we can add other people and needs to our prayer list.

When our church published a prayer calendar to help keep the international ministry family before the congregation, a zealous supporter of prayer and missions asked, "Why do you have only two missionary pictures per month?" (He had hoped we would have at least ten to twelve each month.) I explained, "If we had so many pictures that casual observers felt overwhelmed, what good would that do? We're trying to reach people who are just getting started, and two people are easier to pray for than ten."

We can all start small. Some estimate that 100,000 or more people serve as official "missionaries"—cross-cultural workers sent out by agencies, whether from Western nations or from the emerging mission movements of the majority world. Most of us cannot fathom praying for 100,000 people. But we can handle praying for one or two.

Step 2: Practice Prayer Arrows

The biblical mandate to "pray without ceasing" (1 Thessalonians 5:17 NASB) requires that we try to live in an attitude of prayer. This attitude can include lofting prayer arrows—short prayers offered on the run or in response to an immediate need. Few of us can pray for all the countries of the world. But we can launch a prayer arrow for a country that we hear about in the news, or for an international worker whose name pops into our mind, or for a national church that is facing unusual challenges. I use any means available to help me pray around the world.

The other day I put on a shirt and noticed the label: "Assembled in Mauritius." I stopped to offer arrow prayers for the church in Mauritius, for those who work there as missionaries, and for the spiritual challenges they face. Then I realized how little I knew about Mauritius. So the next day I got my copy of *Operation World* and read specific ways to pray for that island nation.

Other catalysts for launching prayer arrows might include the labels on bananas that identify the country where the bananas were harvested, company names that provoke world-class thoughts such as *Global* Van Lines, or the arrivals/departures screen at the airport, which lists cities of the world. Perhaps sports fans can stop to pray for the countries represented by their favorite players. We can pray at the supermarket for the countries represented in the international-foods section. When we confront something that represents a world outside our own, loft a prayer arrow.

Step 3: Fuel Prayer with Information

The generic "bless the overseas worker" or "guide the church around the world" prayers are far too expansive. We need information about specific people and places to help our prayers. Resources such as operationworld.org as well as newsletters and websites from specific ministries can help us get started praying more intelligently.

One family, who served for more than twenty years in Kenya, told me that they were chagrined to learn while on furlough that people had been praying for their protection from leopards. The missionary responded, "We have been in Kenya eighteen years, and we have prayed to see a leopard without success. In all our years in East Africa, we have never heard of one missionary being attacked by a leopard. Instead, dozens of our friends have been injured or killed in car accidents. We need people to pray about the real dangers we face—like the highways!"

Prayer letters, international periodicals, blogs, websites, or (better yet) direct contact with those working overseas can provide the fuel we need for intelligent, accurate praying. When we pray for our friends in Quito, Ecuador, our first inclination is to think, *They live on the equator in South America; therefore, I'll pray for God to give them grace to withstand the high heat and tropical humidity.* A little information changes our prayer; after we find out that Quito (at 9,000 feet) has year-round daytime temperatures of 70 degrees and nighttime temperatures of 55, we pray, "God, help us not to be jealous of our friends' weather in Quito!"

Step 4: Pray as Part of Our Correspondence

The New Testament Epistles include some excellent prayers on behalf of churches and individuals. In his writings, Paul prayed for these churches. We can do the same as we develop our ministry of correspondence and encouragement to workers and friends in other countries. As we write to them, we can let the Holy Spirit teach us how to pray for them.

Bob Hill, formerly a professor at Greater Europe Mission's Greek Bible Institute in Athens, suggests combining prayer and correspondence: "Keep track of missionaries' current prayer needs and find out what requests have been answered. If you have been praying about something daily for several months, write to ask how the Lord is working with regards to the subject. Ask about special needs. Some items cannot be shared with the general public, and your missionary will appreciate your praying for these needs as well."[3]

Step 5: Participate in the Team Effort of Prayer

While individual intercession is a necessary discipline, group prayer is a powerful tool of God to guide the participants to "agree" together (Matthew 18:19). I'm ashamed of the number of times I've told people I would pray for them and then didn't. Corporate prayer helps me grow in faithfulness. Joining in prayer with brothers and sisters in Christ helps me face the magnitude of the task, because I share the intercession with them.

Dr. Stanley Allaby, former pastor of the Black Rock Congregational Church in Connecticut, told a group of church leaders how he became convinced of the need for faithful, corporate prayer for the overseas family.

> Early in my ministry, we sent out our church's first "home-grown" missionaries. This family was the pride of our missions department. After their first term was over, they returned to our church for a year. At the close of the year, I asked the

husband, "So, Phil, when will you be heading back overseas?" Phil responded, "Pastor, I'm not sure we're going back." "Why not?" I responded. "Well, Pastor, after a year here at the church, I am just not convinced that the church has been and will be praying for us."

Allaby went on to describe his personal repentance and his commitment to lead the church in corporate prayer on behalf of the international family sent by the church. "Through the honesty of that missionary," Allaby concluded, "I became convinced that we must be true to our commitments, because our church family serving in other cultures are depending on us."

Step 6: Find a Personal Plan

When I am inspired to build the discipline of prayer in my life, I'm tempted to copy the person who has motivated me. If sixteenth-century reformer Martin Luther rose at 4:00 AM to pray, then I want to do the same. Imitation is a great learning tool, but we must develop our own patterns for effective prayer. Some pray well as they jog; others need stillness and silence. A few like the idea of all-night prayer vigils once per month. Others do better praying for fifteen consistent minutes every day. We need to find the plan that works best for our lifestyle, metabolism, and spiritual maturity.

One student told me that his prayers for the world Christian movement became consistent when he put a map of the world on the ceiling over his bed. "When I first awake, the map reminds me to pray for the world, starting with the world into which I am sent, but extending beyond my friends to people I pray for in other countries."

The folks at Caleb Resources used a prayer plan that moves from the broadest topics to the most specific. For example, in praying for Muslims in New Delhi, India, start praying at the *macro level* (Muslims worldwide). Then progress inward:

- pray at the *country level* (India)
- pray at the *city level* (New Delhi)
- pray at the *people level* (Muslims as opposed to Hindus)
- pray at the *church level* (the evangelistic efforts of the Indian church)
- pray at the *laborer level* (specific Indian Christians who are trying to reach these Muslims)
- pray at the *personal level* (How does God want me to respond?)[4]

Step 7: Choose Appropriate Tools

Prayer should never be mechanical, but there are tools that can increase our effectiveness in prayer. The tools we choose might be prayer cards of specific missionaries, maps, or pray-around-the-world guides such as *Operation World*. We may also want to think of our prayer posture as a tool. Some of us will choose to intercede in a kneeling posture beside a bed or chair. Others will choose to stand or sit. Some spin a desktop globe and lay hands on the countries. Others investigate on the computer current news stories about the countries, people, or places for which they're praying.

During a recent bout with sleeplessness, I tried a new tool—praying through the alphabet for the world. I focused on the last names of cross-cultural workers I know, beginning with A and praying through the alphabet to Z. I got stuck on X (so I prayed for missionaries who followed the example of Francis Xavier by going to serve in East Asia), but in general, it was a productive prayer time—much more useful than counting sheep.

Another night I decided to pray for countries alphabetically: Algeria, Belgium, Chad, Dominica, Egypt, and so on. The stumpers? Q is limited to Qatar (although I added a prayer for Quito, Ecuador). Z seemed tough until I remembered countries in Africa—Zambia, Zimbabwe, Zaire, and even Zanzibar and Zululand. The toughest again was X; I could not come up with anything. So, in the morning

I looked in a missions dictionary. In the future, I'll remember the Xhosa people of South Africa when I pray through the geographical alphabet.

Step 8: Remember to Intercede

The Pauline prayers found in his letters to the Colossians and the Philippians should guide our intercession. Effective global intercession will mean prayer for spiritual growth, victory in spiritual warfare, and effectiveness in the face of opposition for brothers and sisters around the world. If our petitions are superficial or preoccupied with physical needs, we may never experience the power of answered prayer.

Carl, a missionary for twenty years in South America, lamented after a furlough visit home: "In multiple visits with all of my supporting churches, no one has asked me about my spiritual health, and when I came home last June, my spiritual life was in a state of disrepair. I wasn't praying, my Scripture reading had lapsed, and I was thinking of quitting the ministry. People should never think that because I am a missionary, I am automatically spiritual."

Carl makes a valid point. People who serve in "professional" ministry need prayer for faithfulness in Bible reading, diligence in witnessing, and perseverance in praying. In other words, interceding effectively means praying for them about the same spiritual struggles that we encounter on a daily basis.

Step 9: Pray by Faith—Not by Results

The church in China, the gospel's advance in Muslim countries, and the growth of Christians in little-known areas such as North Korea or Azerbaijan or Mongolia compel us to pray by faith. We commit these places and believers to the Lord—believing that he is at work, even when we do not see it!

When my wife and I took our first trip to East Africa, we experienced some of the results of the great East African revival as we met many men and women who were training for church leadership. In spite of the breakthroughs, however, we sensed a burden to pray for the Maasai people, who, at that point, had been quite resistant to the gospel. Without much information, but with hope, we continued to pray.

Five years later, we began to hear of some breakthroughs, and one year after that, I had the privilege of meeting Mary, a Maasai Christian who served as a schoolteacher. She shared the movement of the Holy Spirit in bringing many Maasai to Jesus Christ.

For Christie and me, it was a lesson in faith—praying for five years concerning people we scarcely knew. But God demonstrated his faithfulness in response to our prayers and the prayers of thousands of others for the Maasai. We remembered to pray at the urge of God's Spirit and not by tangible results.

Step 10: Learn to Say No

If we are to be effective in our intercession, we must learn to stay within our time limitations and our concentration ability. As we pray globally, we will find ourselves besieged with requests to pray more. If we are to be faithful in the priorities that we sense from God, we will need to say no. Most of us cannot pray for thousands of people by name or even hundreds of geographic areas. We need to learn to say no so that we continue to be faithful intercessors in a few areas. In general, faithfulness in prayer leads to fruitfulness in ministry; failure in prayer (committing ourselves to pray for too many people or needs) leads to frustration.

A man called me and asked for a meeting. He wanted to explain his ministry to me in hopes that our church could support him financially. I told him that we had no finances available. He responded, "Well, brother, could I come meet with you so that you could be on my prayer team?" Earlier in my life, I would have said yes, simply out of guilt. But I was just learning this principle of saying no to unrealistic demands. I responded, "Brother, I must tell you the truth. If you came to meet with me, I would pray for you here in my office, but probably not again. I have joined the prayer team of many international workers, and I know I'm not faithful in praying for them. So I must say no to your invitation to be on your team." He was miffed at my honesty, but I determined that I must say no rather than lie by pretending I would pray for him as he asked.

A Worldwide Ministry

Friends in Mozambique asked us to tell the people in our church that they depended on their prayers. The apostle Paul faced turmoil and opposition with confidence because he counted on the Corinthian believers to help him by their prayers.

We face the awesome challenge of helping others in their mission work around the world by supporting them through our prayers. Somewhere in the world, fellow Christians depend on our prayer partnership. Let's do our part to get the job done.[5]

Biblical Texts to Study

- Romans 15:30–32

- 2 Corinthians 1:8–11

- Ephesians 6:18–20

- Philippians 1:12–20

- Colossians 4:2–4

- 2 Thessalonians 3:1

Things to Talk About

- Referencing the Scriptures above, why is it important for us to pray for people involved in world evangelization?

- What obstacles do we face in praying for God's work worldwide?

- How can we respond biblically and practically to those obstacles?

- Read Ephesians 1:15–19; 3:16–19; Philippians 1:9–11; Colossians 1:9–12; and Philemon 6. In what ways can we use Paul's world-class prayers as patterns for our own?

- What goal will you set today to grow in your world-class praying? What steps can you take to accomplish that goal?

A CHANGE IN LIFESTYLE

A world-class Christian's lifestyle is credible in light of what God
wants to do in our world.

Judith Viorst has entertained both children and adults for
almost two decades through her book *Alexander and the Terrible,
Horrible, No Good, Very Bad Day*. At some time or other, we all
identify with poor Alexander as he goes through a difficult day, deal-
ing with gum in his hair, failure in school, the loss of a best friend,
a dessertless lunch, a cavity, a fall in the mud, and lima beans for
dinner. The terrible, horrible, no good, very bad day concludes with
Alexander lamenting:

There was kissing on TV and I hate kissing.

My bath was too hot, I got soap in my eyes, my marble went
down the drain, and I had to wear my railroad-train pajamas.
I hate my railroad-train pajamas.

When I went to bed Nick took back the pillow he said I could
keep, and the Mickey Mouse night-light burned out, and I
bit my tongue.

The cat wants to sleep with Anthony, not with me.

It has been a terrible, horrible, no good, very bad day.[1]

We laugh at Alexander, knowing what a day is like when nothing seems to go right. We see ourselves in his self-pity, which exaggerates lima beans into a reason to move to Australia.

But the repeated theme in the book stimulates a nerve in the world-class Christian. As we laugh our way through Alexander's day, we suddenly hear the title repeated—not for Alexander, but for millions in our world whom we know about through our research, outreach, and prayers.

For millions of people, every day is a terrible, horrible, no good, very bad day. One billion or more people go to bed hungry every evening. Thousands inhabit refugee camps where each day might bring a new disease, intensified suffering, or starvation. Millions live in squalor in our world's cities, some in houses made of cardboard boxes or sheets of aluminum and others scavenging through city dumps in an effort to stay alive.

Our knowledge makes us responsible. As soon as we read about or see these people—for whom every day is terrible, horrible, no good, and very bad—we remember Scripture verses we've studied. We ask ourselves what John means in 1 John 3:17: "If anyone has material possessions and sees his brother in need but has no pity on him, how can the love of God be in him?" Or we wonder what we should do with James's words in James 2:15–17: "Suppose a brother or sister is without clothes and daily food. If one of you says to him, 'Go, I wish you well; keep warm and well fed,' but does nothing about his physical needs, what good is it? In the same way, faith by itself, if it is not accompanied by action, is dead."

These verses, plus our knowledge of worldwide need, usually lead to guilt. And guilt, according to Bob Seiple, former president of World Vision, "is a paralytic emotion." In other words, we feel it, but it leads to inaction. Because we feel helpless, we're paralyzed.

We turn off the television. We throw the mail piece away. Or we react sarcastically: "So what am I supposed to do, send my leftovers to Manila?"

The Biblical Perspective

The combination of our relative affluence (on a global scale) with our awareness of world need calls for some sort of action, and the Scriptures guide our efforts. While a few are called to abandon their riches, all of us are called to stewardship, sacrifice, and solidarity. Let's take a closer look at these three.

Stewardship

Stewardship is understanding that all we have and are belongs to God and that he has assigned us responsibility as caretakers of his wealth. Paul wrote to Timothy about this stewardship perspective: "Command those who are rich in this present world not to be arrogant nor to put their hope in wealth, which is so uncertain, but to put their hope in God, who richly provides us with everything for our enjoyment. Command them to do good, to be rich in good deeds, and to be generous and willing to share. In this way they will lay up treasure for themselves as a firm foundation for the coming age, so that they may take hold of the life that is truly life" (1 Timothy 6:17–19).

Tell the rich people to invest their riches in eternity. Putting hope in wealth makes us think that somehow we can "take it with us." Stewardship is managing in this life the God-given resources for which we will give an account in the next.

Sacrifice

Sacrifice is giving away something that costs us personally. Generosity gives out of abundance, but sacrifice gives when it hurts. Zacchaeus (Luke 19) demonstrated generosity, but the widow who gave her last few cents (Luke 21) demonstrated sacrifice.

The Bible encourages a lifestyle of sacrifice. Killing the lamb without spot or blemish meant sacrificing one of the best of the flock. Imitating Jesus (Philippians 2:5–11) meant following in his voluntary suffering. Offering ourselves as "living sacrifices" (Romans 12:1) implies personal cost of some sort.

Solidarity

Solidarity is taking action to identify ourselves with those in need. The writer of Hebrews sums it up this way: "Remember those in prison as if you were their fellow prisoners, and those who are mistreated as if you yourselves were suffering" (Hebrews 13:3).

Perhaps the greatest call for solidarity is found in Isaiah 58. Through Isaiah, the Lord speaks to correct errant practices of fasting.

> Is not this the kind of fasting I have chosen:
> to loose the chains of injustice
> and untie the cords of the yoke? . . .
> Is it not to share your food with the hungry
> and to provide the poor wanderer with shelter—
> when you see the naked, to clothe him?
> (Isaiah 58:6–7)

He concludes with a promise:

> If you do away with the yoke of oppression . . .
> and if you spend yourselves in behalf of the hungry
> and satisfy the needs of the oppressed,
> then your light will rise in the darkness,
> and your night will become like the noonday.
> (Isaiah 58:9–10)

Fasting in order to identify with the hungry and to help them through our sacrifice is the spirit of solidarity. By our voluntary choice, we become as the hurting persons, assisting them out of our abundance in order to break the cycle of poverty, homelessness, and oppression.

In light of what we know—both about our character as servants of Christ and about the needs of the poor and disenfranchised in our world—we must respond. Jesus calls us to make changes in our lifestyles in order to reflect our perspective as stewards investing in eternity, to make intentional sacrifices in an effort to follow him, and to identify in solidarity with those less fortunate than ourselves.

The biblical bottom line? Jesus calls us to respond to what we know by simplifying our lifestyles.

The Greatest Affluence of All

While visiting a *batey* in the Dominican Republic, I saw economically poor people who had migrated from Haiti, desperate for work. On these Dominican sugar plantations, they were treated like slaves, reduced to nonbeings by a corrupt and greedy system. They were also politically and socially poor, because others had taken away their choices.

In squatter villages on the fringes of many of the world's poorest cities, people arise early in the morning to try to survive another day. They don't ask, "What's for breakfast?" It's either another moldy crust of bread or nothing. They don't stand in front of the closet matching colors and wondering what to wear. They have only one outfit, and if they have two shoes, they are fortunate. Economic conditions have taken away their choices.

The ultimate plight of the poor is that they are without choices. They cannot determine their diet, wardrobe, vocation, or living area. Unlike those of us in affluent areas, they spend little time wondering, *What are my plans for the week, or month, or year?* Their goal is to survive the day.

As we consider simplifying our lifestyles—that is, finding ways to intentionally alter our living patterns so that we might live a more credible kingdom witness—let us pause to thank God for the greatest affluence of all: the affluence of choice.

For some reason God has allowed us to be born into economic abundance; so, we are able to choose our lifestyles. We can choose to simplify. If we move into the gutters of Calcutta to live with that city's 1 million street people, it's our choice. The essence of poverty is to be without choices, and this is poverty few of us will ever experience. Thank God for the affluence of being able to choose to simplify.

Getting Started

Earlier, we said that a world-class Christian lives a credible lifestyle. That is, we live in a way that reflects a global perspective. In light of the vast number of poor and suffering people in our world, we commit ourselves to traveling light—so that we are freer to serve and less encumbered with material concerns.

I wish the Bible offered a specific list of lifestyle requirements: how much money to live on, where to live, when to begin a family, what kind of car to buy, and so on. But it doesn't; and therefore it's difficult for Christians to dogmatically answer these questions. I prefer to focus on issues that call for principled responses before God in each church and in each family.

The Principle of Discernment

We all do well to identify the cultural and economic pressures designed to make us more materialistic. The advertisement from the television set cries to us about 9:00 PM, just after dinner has settled: "Aren't you hungry for a hamburger now?" Our instincts respond, "Yes, I'm hungry now!" And while we may not go out for a hamburger, we may trek to the refrigerator because the television ad just convinced us we were hungry.

The discerning ear identifies the lie and answers, "No, I am in no way hungry. I doubt if I know what it is to feel true hunger." Discernment means recognizing ways the advertising media manipulates us:

- convincing us to make exorbitant expenditures on vacations, face creams, or cars—because we deserve it, we're worth it, or we've earned it
- stimulating us to buy things we're convinced we need, when in reality the word *need* is a euphemism for our greed
- making us feel backward or out of step with the cutting edge of society if we don't own the latest hand-held computer, or jet to tropical destinations, or carry the Gold or Platinum Card

Even the church is not free from being sucked into the materialism of our age. Tom Sine writes, "The standard teaching in most evangelical churches is that you can have as much personal affluence as you want . . . as long as you don't have a materialistic hang-up. Wrong! It's more than an attitude problem. We live in an interconnected, interdependent world. And there is only so much to go around. If I use more than a fair share of the resources God has entrusted to me, someone else is going to go without."[2]

The Principle of Chosen Hardship

The issue of personal sacrifice arises in this principle. If we aspire to live like Jesus, our lives should have an element of chosen hardship, because we desire to grow in character and we want to identify with those less fortunate than ourselves.

Chosen hardship follows the thinking of Ralph Winter, the great missiologist from the U.S. Center for World Mission. He advocates a "wartime, not a peacetime lifestyle" for Christians. Since we are engaged in spiritual warfare for the souls of people, Dr. Winter encourages everyone to cut back, even as every citizen made personal sacrifices during wartime in an effort to support the national cause.

If more Christians do not choose at least some hardship, the task of world evangelization will never be accomplished. Patrick Johnstone, coauthor of *Operation World*, writes, "This denial of self and a willingness to embrace all the implications of discipleship flies in the face of twentieth century North American culture. Unless we are willing for this, we will never get the job done. I fear many are using ways to try to evangelize that avoid the Cross."[3]

But what does "chosen hardship" mean to you and me? A Sunday school class came up with the following suggestions:

- choose to camp on vacation rather than stay in a hotel, so we can feel what it is to live that way (real camping—with tents, open fires, lanterns—not living in a Winnebago with all the comforts of home)
- work in one ministry or service per month—in obscurity (something no one knows about except Jesus)
- give away something you know you don't need (or you know someone else who needs it more than you)
- walk to work or take public transportation to save money on gas
- skip one meal per week, saving the money to donate to a relief agency
- serve a holiday meal at a soup kitchen

Elizabeth Brewster, professor at Fuller School of Intercultural Studies, articulated the lifestyle of chosen hardship in solidarity with the poor through the "Zaccheus Covenant," distributed at Lausanne II, the Second International Congress on World Evangelization (Manila, 1989):

To implement the statements on the poor in the Lausanne Covenant and the Manila Manifesto, I covenant to

• fast and pray weekly or monthly as a sign of my identification with the poor and my desire for their salvation and transformation (Isaiah 58:5–8);

• regularly review my possessions, purchasing, housing, transportation, recreation, professional equipment, and expenses in order to develop a simpler life style (1 Timothy 6:6–8);

• learn from the poor through visiting, worshiping the Lord with them, working alongside them, and becoming friends with them (John 1:14);

• speak up for the poor in defense of their rights, even at risk to myself (Proverbs 31:8–9);

• continually encourage my church or mission agency to proclaim the Lord Jesus to the poor, to plant and develop Christ's church among them, to give compassionately, and to work for the removal of the causes of their poverty (Luke 4:18);

• annually review my commitment to this covenant with a friend to whom I will make myself accountable (Luke 19:8).

Signed _____

Dated _____

The Principle of Not Buying on Impulse

One of the greatest hazards of credit cards is the removal of economic limitation. "If I can charge it, I can afford it." This attitude caters to greed, carelessness, and a host of other bad motives that provoke us to buy things on impulse. With credit cards, we don't need to plan, budget, or think through our decisions.

Impulse buying leads to one of two negative outcomes: Either we live beyond our means (because we owe for things purchased on impulse), or we find ourselves owning things we don't need (in the same way that we find junk food in our grocery bag when shopping before dinner).

One world-class Christian told me that one of his lifestyle choices includes "not wandering through the mall during my free time." He said, "When I go through the mall with credit cards in my wallet, I am tempted to buy things just because they look attractive. To wean myself from impulse buying, I take a walk down the street, not through the mall."

The Principle of Not Buying If Sharing Is Possible

Our society is built on a foundation of individual ownership, but responsible use of our resources should call some of this into question. For example, could families in a neighborhood share one lawn mower, since it's usually used no more than once a week per family? Do we all have to own our own freezers, or could households buy one large freezer to use together? Can we save money by forming a neighborhood or church cooperative for buying food?

These ideas on sharing introduce us to other tough questions: Who services the mower? How do we pay for the electricity used by the freezer? What if the buyer in the cooperative purchases food we don't want? The issue, however, is not ease; the issue is voluntary simplicity, and this may lead our churches to greater discovery of both working together in community and developing an attitude of openhandedness toward our possessions. Simplifying one's life will always seem an encumbrance to a society bent on personal comfort.

The Principle of Staying Out of Debt

Is it possible in our world to stay out of debt? When we read biblical statements such as "Let no debt remain outstanding, except the continuing debt to love one another" (Romans 13:8) or "The borrower becomes the lender's slave" (Proverbs 22:7 NASB), we surge with desire to stay out of debt. But then we start the process of buying a home, or we receive the tuition bill for a college education. Debt free? Tell me how!

Whether it's possible to stay debt free is not the issue for most people. The issue is the epidemic of debt that has swept our world. Just when we start to get all of our credit card debt paid off, some bank sends us a new Visa card in the mail with a $1,500 line of credit. We spend beyond our means and then pay 18 percent interest or more to bail ourselves out.

A simpler life may mean destroying credit cards or, perhaps more realistically, determining to pay each month's statement in full. With many families in the United States living a lifestyle approaching a level 110 to 120 percent of their income, growing toward simplicity will take time and discipline. In the long run, simple living frees both the individual and the financial resources to stay clear of debt.

Every Christian and every church need to do some hard thinking on this issue of debt. Some churches have determined not to build new buildings until all of the funds have been raised. Others pool their resources to help students go to college, especially those who are anticipating full-time Christian service. The issue of stewardship arises again: What is the best way for me to manage the resources with which God has entrusted me?[4]

The Principle of Beating the System

My wife and I enjoy finding ways around the economic pressures of our world. Hunting for bargains, using coupons, and looking for deals can help us acquire the things we need without being extravagant in expenditures.

When we were engaged, Christie started looking for a wedding gown. Several of our friends had spent in excess of $1,000 for theirs. But no matter how romantic we felt, we simply could not rationalize such an expenditure for the sake of a six-hour afternoon. We prayed about it, and Christie went bargain hunting. The result? A beautiful gown from Filene's Basement in Boston—for $29.

As a leader in Sunday worship during my seminary days, I needed a suit. But I had no suit and little money to buy one. Again, we prayed. Then we headed off to a "railroad salvage" warehouse to start shopping. For only $25 I bought a Pierre Cardin suit that looked tailored specifically for me and perfectly met my needs.

Beat the system. Used cars, discount outlets, volume buying through cooperatives, and thorough research before purchasing can enhance our stewardship and cut back our spending. In the process, we can have fun.

Many Christians feel the greatest pressure of materialism around the Christmas holidays. Advertising makes us feel that our love for others is directly measured by how much we spend on them, and yet each year we ask ourselves, "Why did we spend so much this year?" Why not beat that system and get into creative giving at Christmas?

Many organizations now offer annual alternative-gift catalogs that include gifts for the homeless, sick, and needy. Instead of buying many gifts for the person who needs none, consider giving one of the following to someone in need:

- $60 buys one year's tuition to a Child Care Center for a Palestinian child on the West Bank

- $5 feeds for one day a hungry person at an urban or rural food pantry in the United States
- $1 buys five pounds of seed to help start a farm in Ethiopia or Somalia
- $4 buys a piglet in Thailand ($40 for a pig); $10 buys a flock of ten ducks in Mozambique
- $1 buys ten tree seedlings in Haiti, all life-giving gifts to someone in need

The Principle of Right Motives

Addressing the issues of things, possessions, and "stuff" forces us to confront our motives. How owned are we? Are we so owned by our things that we cannot share? How much value do we attach to our possessions? Do we equate our worth with owning? Tom Sine writes, "Whatever commands our time, energy, and resources, commands us."[5]

Scott Wesley Brown's song "Things" poignantly addresses our love of possessions. Read the following words slowly:

Things upon the mantle,
Things on every shelf.
Things that others gave me,
Things I gave myself.
Things I've stored in boxes
That don't mean much anymore,
Old magazines and memories
Behind the attic door.

Things on hooks and hangers,
Things on ropes and rings.
Things I guard that blind me to
The pettiness of things.
Am I like the Rich Young Ruler,
Ruled by all I own?

If Jesus came and asked me,
Could I leave them all alone?

Oh Lord, I look to heaven,
Beyond the veil of time,
To gain eternal insight
That nothing's really mine,
And to only ask for daily bread
And all contentment brings,
To find freedom as
Your servant in the midst of all these things.

For discarded in the junkyards,
Rusting in the rain,
The things that took the finest years
Of lifetimes to obtain.
And whistling through these tombstones,
The hollow breezes sing
A song of dreams surrendered to
The tyranny of things.[6]

The World-Class Christian Spirit

Many people will arise today to live a terrible, horrible, no good, very bad day. But we can act to do something in response. We can choose to live more simply so that others may simply live. There is enough to go around. But sharing our abundance with others calls us to cut back somewhere, to limit ourselves voluntarily, to live a lifestyle that reflects our knowledge of the condition of people in our world.

The credible lifestyle and spirit of a world-class Christian display contentment, stewardship, sacrifice, and solidarity.

Two things I ask of you, O LORD; do not refuse me
    before I die:

Keep falsehood and lies far from me;

give me neither poverty nor riches, but give me only
my daily bread.

Otherwise, I may have too much and disown you and
say,

"Who is the LORD?"

Or I may become poor and steal, and so dishonor the
name of my God.

(Proverbs 30:7–9)

Biblical Texts to Study

- Scriptures regarding *stewardship*
  Psalm 24:1

  Matthew 6:19–21

  Mark 4:18–19

  1 Timothy 6:17–20

- Scriptures regarding *sacrifice*
  Luke 21:1–4

  2 Corinthians 8:1–5

- Scriptures regarding *solidarity*

  Deuteronomy 15:7–8

  Proverbs 19:17

  Isaiah 58:6–10

  Hebrews 13:3

Things to Talk About

- Referencing the Scriptures above, describe biblical stewardship, sacrifice, and solidarity.

- Are these three qualities vital to living a credible world-Christian lifestyle? Why?

- What obstacles might a world-Christian lifestyle present to us? To our households? How might we respond biblically and practically to these obstacles?

- Considering the inequities of our world, does "chosen hardship" imply "chosen poverty"?

• What elements of the Zaccheus Covenant might your own covenant of chosen hardship contain?

• What goal will you set today to grow in living a world-Christian lifestyle? What steps can you take to accomplish that goal?

MONEY:
AT THE HEART OF THE MATTER

God loves a cheerful giver.

THE APOSTLE PAUL

Some television personalities promote a "health and wealth" gospel, which teaches that God intends to make every Christian wealthy, healthy, and prosperous. Their themes focus around God as some sort of celestial ATM: just figure out the right formula, and blessings, healing, deliverance, and success will pour out. For these teachers, wealth becomes identical to God's blessing, and the love of money equals the love of experiencing God's best.

Dr. Barry, on the other hand, teaches that *money* is the root of all evil, rather than *the love of money*, which the Scripture teaches in 1 Timothy 6:10. He looks at the rich of our world and responds in pious disgust, "Well, they may be rich, but they aren't happy." When asked why rich people seem so happy, he says it's a result of their perverse minds.

I grew up in Christian churches where this attitude was taught, and as I grew, it was a troubling paradox to me to find that some of these incredibly affluent people were both happy and generous.

While I agreed that money could not buy happiness, poverty didn't seem to guarantee happiness either.

We Christians fluctuate in a love-hate relationship with money. One group implies an approval of selfishness and greed, where givers make deals with God—giving ten dollars away in hopes of getting one hundred in return from the slot machines of heaven. The other group implies a disdain for money, making the handling of money, one of our most basic stewardships, into an unavoidable evil that is managed begrudgingly.

The biblical perspective of the world-class Christian lies between these two extremes. The television prosperity preachers teach a partial truth, because God does sometimes bless people with economic gain as a result of living by biblical standards. Abraham certainly was wealthy, as were King David, Solomon, and some of the people who supported Jesus' ministry. But there is no absolute rule.[1] If there were, the godliest people of the world would live in Beverly Hills or on Fifth Avenue in Manhattan, and the most unspiritual people would live in abject poverty. Experience in the global church teaches us that this is far from true.

Dr. Barry, however, does make a legitimate biblical point: Money should never be taken lightly. Of the thirty-seven New Testament parables (many pertaining to the kingdom of heaven), seventeen concern money, property, or stewardship. Managing our resources is certainly important to Jesus. The evil attached to greed cannot be dismissed as insignificant. The apostle Paul writes with intensity to Timothy: "People who want to get rich fall into temptation and a trap and into many foolish and harmful desires that plunge men into ruin and destruction. For the love of money is a root of all kinds of evil. Some people, eager for money, have wandered from the faith and pierced themselves with many griefs" (1 Timothy 6:9–10).

The toughest monetary issue facing us is that of *stewardship*. How can we manage the financial resources that God has put at our disposal? How can we stay balanced so that we neither venerate wealth as the sign of our obedience nor diminish it to a crude evil force?

Two truths characterize world-class Christian giving: (1) God calls us to be generous in our giving, and (2) God calls us to be responsible in our giving. These truths lead to two subsequent questions: Why should we be generous? and How can we give wisely?

Why Be Generous?

Generosity. Liberality. Openhandedness. Munificence. These words should characterize the Christian who realizes the abundance that God has given us, especially in the affluent Western world. Because we have so much, we can choose both to simplify and to be generous.

And yet, when the topic of money arises, the questions I'm asked include "Should I tithe (give 10 percent) before or after taxes?" "Do I need to give money away from the profits on my investments, or can I limit it to just my salary?" "Can I include donations to nonprofit organizations that are not uniquely Christian to bring me up to 10 percent?" "Should I ever give a gift of money if it's not tax deductible?"

While these questions have some legitimacy, those who ask them have missed the biblical point of generosity. God calls us to be generous, and through generosity, we grow. If we spend our energy trying to figure out how to give the bare minimum and still be obedient Christians, we miss the freedom that accompanies generosity.

Our Attitude

Generosity affects our attitudes. Remember Charles Dickens's character Ebenezer Scrooge? When he lived as a miser, he was rich, alone, and grumpy. But when he was transformed by his vision of the future, he overflowed with generosity, and his entire outlook on life changed. Suddenly Scrooge's wealth became to him a tool for enriching the happiness of others, and when he gave, his joy was multiplied many times over.

When we are transformed by our vision of the future—investing our lives now for eternity—we cannot help but be generous. Our perspective changes. We see that everything comes as a gift from God, and it's now our privilege to use our resources to enrich the lives of others.

Generosity increases our joy because it frees us. It releases us from the grip of money because we have courage to give it away. In days of economic uncertainty, many spend precious emotional energy worrying about the future. They fear either not getting what they want or losing what they have. Generosity puts our lives into a wider arena. We take our eyes off ourselves and realize that God is our provider and that he will take care of us.

Bernie grew up in poverty, but through the diligence of his father and his siblings, his extended family became wealthy. In the process, Bernie became a Christian, and one of the first areas that the Lord touched in his life was money. To help Bernie from becoming possessive or greedy, God taught him generosity.

Bernie is very wealthy, but he is free from it. He lives with an openhanded generosity, giving away in excess of 50 percent of his income. He gives liberally of both money and time, serving in his church and around the world. He retired early so that he could be free to serve. Bernie provides a sharp contrast to his siblings, who criticize their brother. They hoard their money and remain tight-fisted, fearing they might lose it and return to the poverty of their childhood.

Our Perspective

Generosity affects our perspective of ourselves in the world. As Christ's ambassadors, we always look for ways to make known our loyalty to him. Giving should never be used as some sort of pharisaic self-aggrandizement, but it does set us apart from the world in which we live. Our monetary habits make it clear that we are walking out of step with the values of our world.

C. S. Lewis articulated our distinctiveness from the rest of society in his book *Mere Christianity*: "Charity—giving to the poor—is an essential part of Christian morality: in the frightening parable of the sheep and the goats, it seems to be the point on which everything else turns." He continues by describing how such charity ought to set us apart from our neighbors:

> I am afraid the only safe rule [about how much to give] is to give more than we can spare. In other words, if our expenditure on comforts, luxuries, amusements, etc., is up to the standard common among those with the same income as our own, we are probably giving away too little. If our charities do not at all pinch or hamper us, I should say they are too small. There ought to be things we should like to do and cannot do because our charitable expenditures exclude them.[2]

Generous giving affects our perspective of ourselves in the world. When others might buy without restraint, we find self-control, because as Christians, we commit ourselves to generosity. Lewis points out that even if generosity is not noticeable to our neighbors, it will be known to us because it will "pinch us" and keep us from living up to the economic standard of those who earn the same amount we do.

"Keeping up with the neighbors" will not be possible if we see ourselves as followers of Christ and live out this commitment in our giving patterns.

Our Worship

Generosity affects our worship. Arranging regular electronic bank withdrawals or writing a weekly or monthly check to the church or ministry we support is an act of worship, because it teaches us that everything belongs to God, and we act as his stewards.

Our church services should emphasize more giving gifts as part of corporate worship. Too many Sunday worshipers view the offering plate as some sort of church membership dues, admission fee, or obligation. Instead, giving worshipfully acknowledges our gratitude to and expresses our dependency on God our provider.

Dr. Haddon Robinson highlights giving as worship because it reflects before God our attitude and level of sacrifice. "I believe God honors many poor people who don't give a tenth," Robinson writes, "because what they do give is a sacrificial amount in relationship to what they earn. Similarly, for many wealthy people, giving a tenth is a way of robbing God. Their tithe becomes a tip."[3]

Giving addresses a fundamental aspect of our worship. We kneel, physically demonstrating our submission to God. We hear the Word of God preached, symbolic of our commitment to live under its authority. We give, demonstrating to ourselves and to God the understanding that our resources belong to him.

Art recently became a Christian, and part of his growth has been learning the joy of generosity. After hearing of a need in our church family, he wrote a check to cover the expenses related to the need. He told me, "Giving gives me a unique sense of partnership with Jesus. Since I have become a Christian, my whole outlook on my money has changed. Now I see that God has entrusted money to me so that he can touch other people's lives through me. Every week, deciding how to give more is spiritually exhilarating."

Our World

Generosity affects our world. Art reflects the fact that God wants to transform our world and the needs around us through our generosity. As stewards of God's money, we have incredible opportunities to affect our world and the advance of the gospel.

Chuck and Debbie, a young two-career couple, wanted to use their wealth for the kingdom of Christ. They had purchased a new car several years earlier, and now it was paid off. They told me, "We don't want to buy any more new cars, but we would like to use our monthly car payments to support an overseas ministry."

Instead of spending the monthly payments on themselves, Chuck and Debbie took the amount they had been paying on their car and gave it to a ministry that supported national evangelists in majority-world countries. Their monthly gift supports an evangelist and his family, and their generosity has enabled the evangelist to be free of monetary concerns so that he could plant three new churches in a predominantly Muslim country. Individuals, families, and churches multiply their own joy of giving when they discover ways to use generous stewardship to affect the world.

How to Give Wisely

"Who can I trust?" The words came from a generous giver at our church. He had read in a newspaper another tale of embezzlement and financial mismanagement in the religious world. He continued: "I want to give—and give generously—but how do I know that my money will get where I send it? How do I know what reports to believe? How can I be sure that I am not being duped by some dynamic personality?"

Giving makes us vulnerable. We could give money away and then find that it was misused. That is one of the risks of giving. But we can take some helpful steps to keep from making mistakes with the money we desire to invest in the work of Christ.

Step 1: Give through the Local Church

Our own fellowship, the place where we "belong," is the best place to start giving. The local church allows us to integrate our giving with our worship, and it provides a system of accountability by which we can monitor how our dollars are being used.

When I give to my local church, I support the ministry that edifies me each week. Some people call this "storehouse tithing," giving the first 10 percent to the local congregation to which they are committed. Giving to the local church allows me to see where the money is spent. If the pastor is driving a Mercedes, I'll know it. If the church is avoiding missions and spending money only on itself, I'll read about it in the annual report.

Giving to the local church also encourages my involvement in it. When it is my stewardship being expended, I pay more attention to the missions strategy of the church and to the staff members the church employs. Involvement is another way to help manage my stewardship giving.

Tom Sine challenges every local church giver: "Local churches need to make an evaluation. I encourage them to do an audit of where their time and money goes. In the churches I work with, 80 percent of the time and money stays right in the building. Tom Skinner has said we tithe to ourselves—we put money back in buildings, programs, and facilities. If we're serious about the Great Commission and the Great Commandment, we should set a goal of at least 50 percent of the time and money going to causes outside the church building."[4]

The church exists for the benefit of its nonmembers. When we give to the local church, we can help make sure such an outward focus persists.

Step 2: Give Regularly

In teaching the Corinthians about giving, Paul wrote, "On the first day of every week, each one of you should set aside a sum of money in keeping with his income" (1 Corinthians 16:2). Paul clearly teaches them the discipline of consistent giving.

Some prefer to give monthly and some prefer quarterly, but the principle is the same: Disciplined giving will do the most good to us (reinforcing the fact that our money belongs to God) and to the people or organizations we support (providing them with regular income).

Regular giving is in contrast to impulse giving. Solicitations for money come to us through infomercials, direct-mail advertisements, and even sidebars on websites because of Americans' propensity to give on impulse. A fundraiser from Oxfam America told me that over 90 percent of American households give something to charitable causes, but many of these do so upon impulse. A British fundraiser for a Christian relief organization reiterated this reality when he observed that "Americans are simultaneously the most generous and the most impulsive givers I have ever met." While impulse giving might achieve the budgetary goals of nonprofit organizations, it loses the impact on us because we give without forethought, discipline, and worship.

Step 3: Give Strategically

Whether on the personal or the local church level, we do best by giving according to a plan. None of us can afford to give something to everything, so we need (as individuals and as churches) to decide where we can make our greatest, most strategic impact.

One of my friends has prioritized the work of Bible translation with the Wycliffe Bible Translators. His strategy focuses on getting the Bible translated into languages that currently have no Bible. He implements his strategy by getting involved in his church's international outreach committee and by encouraging his church to include Bible translation in its overall giving strategy. He also concentrates the money that he gives outside of the local church on the work of Wycliffe.

Some focus their giving on the urban poor in the United States. Others favor education. Supporting majority-world leaders attracts some, while others give to an issue-specific ministry, such as radio ministry (HCJB Global, Quito, Ecuador), efforts to resettle refugees (World Relief), or efforts to combat human trafficking (International Justice Mission).

Influenced by vast needs worldwide, every person and church can be tempted to spread their giving throughout the world. Churches that boast of three hundred missionaries in one hundred countries may be too concerned with having multiple names listed on their "Global Family" map. As a result, they spread their support too thin. Strategic giving means deciding where we would like to have a substantial impact rather than simply giving broadly. Even the largest churches understand this concept. To achieve the most impact, Saddleback Church strategically focuses its energy in Rwanda, and Willow Creek Church works intensely with World Vision in the Dominican Republic.

Step 4: Get Involved with Giving

Giving should not be reduced to an impersonal exercise in exchanging checks for receipts. We need to get involved, when possible, with the people and ministries we support.

Getting involved means researching, reading carefully through reports and newsletters, and supporting people in prayer as well as through monetary gifts. Getting involved might mean going on campus to see "in action" the InterVarsity staff person we support. It could mean participating in a Habitat for Humanity building project to which we give support. In some cases, it means a trip overseas to visit a missionary or a national Christian leader we support. Such a visit might be costly, but it usually results in tremendous financial response, because we enjoy giving to ministries and people whose work we have seen firsthand.

The strongest internationally focused churches link involvement and giving. One church endeavors, over a yearlong period, to get an overseas ministry partner into every church member's home. Another church features overseas exposure trips each year for about fifty members, introducing them personally to cross-cultural ministry. A third church does a pulpit and choir exchange once per year with an inner-city partner church so that these churches that give to each other's ministries will know each other personally.

Step 5: Give Cautiously

Several years ago, my wife and I began giving to ministries in South Africa. We started receiving more solicitations (because some organizations sell their donor lists to each other), and one group caught our attention. A polished brochure boasted of incredible successes in ministry at remarkably low costs. On impulse, I was ready to write a check, but my wife exhorted a more careful look.

The closer we looked at the organization, the more questions arose: Why did the director own two homes? Why were there three members of the president's family on a board with seven members? Why were they supporting a man who was in political trouble because of his racist views?

Our questions led to a personal meeting with the president. When our inquiries were met with defensiveness and hostility, our fears intensified. We decided not to be involved in giving to that ministry.

Whenever we consider giving to a church or ministry, we should ask questions. Does the agency belong to ECFA—the Evangelical Council for Financial Accountability, a group dedicated to helping Christian organizations maintain financial integrity? If not, then we ask questions such as:

- How are workers and programs financed?
- If we give to a project, especially an overseas relief project, what percentage of our dollar goes toward the project to which we've given?
- How much of the amount raised by individual workers is salary? What is the overhead, and where does the rest go?
- Are contributions to the organization tax deductible?

- To what national accrediting or overseeing organizations does the agency belong?
- Are the financial records audited each year?
- Who makes up the board, and how accountable is the president to the board?

Being cautious does not mean being suspicious. It simply means thinking of our giving as an investment and investigating the work of the agency as we would any bank or institution that manages our financial accounts.

World-Class Giving

Dr. Haddon Robinson tells a story of his early days of raising funds for Denver Seminary, where he served as president. He approached a businessman with a financial need of $20,000 for a new phone system. The businessman asked, "How much would you like me to give?" Robinson, not wanting to be presumptuous, asked, "Could you give $1,000?"

The businessman wrote out the check, and as he handed it over, he told Robinson, "You insulted me." The comment stunned Robinson, so the businessman continued: "You asked me for $1,000, but you needed $20,000. Either you felt that I wasn't able to give much money, in which case you underestimated where I am financially, or worse, you thought I had the money but wouldn't give you more, in which case you insulted my generosity."[5]

Dr. Robinson left that meeting vowing never to underestimate the power of God to work through his people to meet great financial needs. That businessman, a world-class giver, was waiting to respond to the challenge of generosity.

We might not have $20,000 in our checkbooks waiting to be given away, but we all have some resources over which we serve as stewards. Utilizing our money to the glory of God is essential to world-class Christian discipleship.

"Remember this: Whoever sows sparingly will also reap sparingly, and whoever sows generously will also reap generously. Each man should give what he has decided in his heart to give, not reluctantly or under compulsion, for God loves a cheerful giver" (2 Corinthians 9:6–7).

Biblical Texts to Study

- 1 Corinthians 16:1–2

- 2 Corinthians 8:1–6

- 2 Corinthians 8: 7–15

- 2 Corinthians 9:6–15

Things to Talk About

- Have you ever received from someone a gift that was sacrificially given? What were the giver's motives and attitudes in giving? What responses or results came from that act of giving?

- Referencing the Scriptures above, what does the apostle Paul teach about right attitudes, motives, and acts of giving? What are the results of giving with right attitudes?

• What does the apostle Paul teach about wrong attitudes, motives, and acts of giving? What are the results of giving with wrong attitudes?

• What is the relationship between what God has done for us and our giving to spread the gospel?

• How does generosity affect our attitudes? Our perspectives? Our worship? The world?

• Read 1 Chronicles 29:14. How should this verse transform our giving?

• What changes in your attitudes, motives, or actions related to giving will help you grow as a world-class Christian?

REACHING THE WORLD THAT HAS COME TO US

The alien living with you must be treated as one of your native-born. Love him as yourself.

LEVITICUS 19:34

The visit to the hospital that night in October commenced an ordeal that would last for eight months. My mother-in-law was admitted and began a series of surgeries, recuperations, setbacks, and rebounds that would continue into May.

For the family, those months were times of waiting, praying, and hanging around the hospital. When the most difficult times were over, we were still spending almost every free evening visiting her.

I soon began to ask myself, *Here I am locked into a schedule that brings me to the hospital all the time. How can I build a world-class vision in this environment?*

As I overheard two hospital workers from Haiti speaking to each other in Creole, an idea came to me: *Why not initiate more conversations with other patients and hospital employees, especially those with foreign accents?*

Over the next few months, I met many men and women from Haiti, several workers from El Salvador, one from Nicaragua, another from Israel. There was an emergency room doctor from Saudi Arabia, an anesthesiologist from Bombay, a medical school student from Gabon, and a nurse from Mozambique. We met others from England, Portugal, Colombia, Germany, and Japan. In the hallways of one Boston hospital, we grew in our understanding of the global village in which we live.

Our experiences in that hospital reminded us that world-class Christian involvement does not start overseas. It starts by looking for and reaching out to the world that God has brought to us.

The Melting Pot Reality

What country has the second largest black population? How about the fourth largest Spanish-speaking nation in the world? What country has the second largest Polish city, the largest Jewish population, the second largest Puerto Rican city, the second largest Hispanic population center, and some of the largest Haitian, Cuban, Dominican, and Guatemalan cities in the world?

According to Jerry Appleby, in *Missions Have Come to America*, the answer to all of these questions is the United States.[1] Only Nigeria has a larger black population. Some argue that the United States has overtaken Argentina as the third largest Spanish-speaking country. Chicago's Polish population is second only to Warsaw, and there are more Jews in New York City than in Tel Aviv. With hundreds of thousands of new immigrants each year, the United States has become one of the most international places on earth.

One pastor put it this way: "God called us to go into all the world, but we didn't do it. So God brought all the world to us." A United Nations worker estimated that the United States is perhaps the only country on earth where someone from every country on earth lives.

The newest members of the melting pot come to us for three reasons: as students, as immigrants, and as refugees.

International Students

International students from around the world pass through U.S. Customs each year to pursue undergraduate and graduate degrees. Many come from countries where Christian ministry is limited, and they come with stereotypes of the United States as a "Christian" country.

Lawson Lau, an international student ministry specialist, describes international students this way: "Temporarily uprooted from familiar social, economic, cultural, and religious surroundings, tens of thousands of international students are transplanted each year onto the soil of colleges and universities in the United States. The frontiers of foreign missions are no longer only in Tibet, Saudi Arabia, Mongolia, and China. They are also in Boston, New York, Chicago, and Los Angeles, for they have come to the United States in the presence of international visitors."[2]

Sadly, only a fraction of these international students ever visit an American home during their time here. As a result, they return to their countries either desperately lonely and bitter about their isolation while in America or disillusioned by the thought that dormitory life exemplified the lifestyle of "Christian" America.

Several years ago, my brother-in-law Bob died at age forty-seven of a heart attack. He had never married, so Christie and I became executors of his estate, a process that included going through all of his possessions. We found his 1973 Harvard University yearbook, and as we scanned for his picture, we were fascinated to learn that he had been a classmate with Benazir Bhutto, a young woman from one of the most powerful families in Pakistan. She eventually became prime minister of Pakistan, and before her assassination, she was regarded as one of the most influential women in the Muslim world. Looking at her picture, we wondered if, during her time in the United States, any Christian had reached out to her. Was she welcomed into someone's home? Or did she return to Pakistan thinking the wild dorm life of the 1970s was representative of "Christian" America?

The leaders of International Students, Inc. (ISI) estimate that as many as 75 percent of all international students studying in the United States never enter an American home. Gordon Loux, former president of ISI, articulated his dream that "every international student will have one Christian friend." May we carry out his dream of international students returning to their homelands having learned through our lives of Christ.

Immigrants

The second large group of newcomers to the United States is *immigrants*. Education, world travel, international business, and the desire for a better life (economically) have led many internationals to make the United States their home. In Boston, for example, there are an estimated 100,000 Haitians, which is less than half the size of "Little Haiti" in Miami (which is much smaller than "Little Havana").

In our little town of Lexington, Massachusetts, I buy donuts from men and women from the Azores and Brazil. Large numbers of Indian and Chinese families move in regularly. The Indian restaurant in town has pictures of the owner's favorite Hindu deities, and the Thai restaurant across the street has statues of the Buddha holding food offerings. And one day after the adult swim ended at our town pool, I saw four boys come in together for their afternoon swim: one Caucasian, one black, one Indian, and one Asian. In these four friends, I could see the international scope of the youth of our town.

And city life is even more diverse. The Southern Baptists have planted ethnic-specific churches around Boston to reach out to Haitians, Hispanics, Cambodians, Laotians, Greeks, and Arabic-speaking people. A friend of mine pastors a New York City church where fifteen languages are spoken. Ray Bakke, a renowned urban specialist, once observed that over ninety languages are spoken in his home city of Chicago—a scenario that could be repeated in Los Angeles, New York, and Atlanta.

Like international students, many of these immigrants come from Muslim, Hindu, Buddhist, or even communist countries where they have never heard the gospel. Yet, when in the United States, they find themselves isolated and alone. Some of the poorest immigrants come from so-called Christian countries with no proper documentation, just an earnest desire for a better life for themselves and their families. How we, as world-class Christians, respond to newcomers from around the world will demonstrate if we believe in God's love for *all* people through Jesus Christ.

Refugees

The third cluster of newcomers is *refugees*. Some estimate that as many as 1 million refugees enter the United States each year. Canada, Australia, and European countries welcome thousands of others. These are political or economic exiles from the Middle East, Central America, and Southeast Asia—or any place where turmoil might drive them out.

Refugees represent a special call to the church of Jesus Christ, because they are truly the "aliens and strangers" of our world. Homeless, displaced, and alone, these people will respond with unique openness to the love of Jesus demonstrated through his people.

The refugees now in our midst might otherwise never hear the gospel. A group of Laotian refugees from a mountain tribe that is classified as a "hidden people group" has been displaced to a community in the northwest United States where the gospel is freely preached. Christians in that area can reach people who have eluded missions outreach for decades in their own country.

Reaching Internationals—Practical Ideas

Bill and Judy have become missionaries to all of the People's Republic of China, simply by opening their home to international students who come to their area for six months of training. And Scott has a friendship evangelism ministry that affects Saudi Arabia, one of the most restricted Muslim countries in the world. Scott has also moved into a Boston neighborhood where all of his neighbors are from Morocco, another Muslim nation. Steve is reaching many from East Asia because he's willing to spend three hours every Saturday morning tutoring immigrants who desire to learn English. Chris helped a Christian graduate student from East Africa understand and respond to the secularist viewpoint of his professors by inviting him to join a Bible study.

Finding opportunities for outreach doesn't require an enormous amount of creative genius; we only need to look around us, open our lives and our homes, and try to be friends. Kathy Lay and her husband used unemployment as an outreach opportunity to internationals: "When my husband was laid off from work three years ago, he frequented a small donut shop near the unemployment office. Once a week for four months he talked with the Korean owner. Three years later we are still friends with him. We were the only Americans invited to his wedding, we prayed with him as his wife delivered their son, and we have spent time with them socially and in Bible Study."[3]

All forms of outreach to internationals build on at least three principles: prayer, learning, and friendship.

Principles for Outreach: Prayer

First, start on a *foundation of prayer*. Bill and Judy pray for opportunities to meet people living in their community from the People's Republic of China. Then they hang out at the Chinese vegetable section of their supermarket. One group of five Chinese seemed especially prepared by God. When Bill and Judy befriended them, they said, "We have two questions. First, can you help us use the public transportation? And second, we would like to go to a church; could you take us to church?"

Tom and Carolyn build on a similar foundation of prayer, and they open their house to international tenants. God has brought them Buddhist students from Malaysia, communist students from China, and Muslim students from Egypt. In each case, the students God has brought to them have been very open to discussions about Jesus, and one who became a Christian is returning to his family and country with a desire to evangelize.

Don and Meg prayed for years for their Pakistani Muslim friend. She was warm to their friendship but resistant to the gospel, so they prayed. After six years of friendship, prayer, and occasional discussions about the person of Jesus, their friend put her faith in Christ.

After praying, a church in Southern California decided to get involved with the hundreds of undocumented Mexican immigrants in their community. Some members started an English as a Second Language class. Others looked into the immigration process and retained a Christian immigration lawyer to help create a "safe place" for these newcomers to start the appropriate paperwork for immigration.

Principles for Outreach: Friendship

Second, build on *friendship*. Friendship is the single most important ingredient in reaching out to internationals.[4] They need friends who will help them grow comfortable with the confusing culture of the United States. One friend spent a morning orienting a family of refugees on how to use an American home—from electric stoves to flush toilets, which were unlike anything they had ever seen.

Reaching out to internationals does not require an unusual gift of evangelism; it demands only a willingness to be a friend. Many internationals come from family-oriented cultures, and they need us to invite them into our families. When Norm and Debbie invited his co-worker from India over for pizza, they met his entire family. In the course of conversation, Norm and Debbie discovered that although this man and his family had been in the United States for five years, Norm and Debbie's home was the first American home this family had visited. Until that friendship started, the Indian family had depended on television to teach them about American family life!

Gordon Loux writes, "International students in the United States are particularly vulnerable to loneliness and the disruption of a new culture. They need friends who can help them adjust to American life, answer practical questions, and ease the loneliness of separation from friends and family."[5]

Here are some practical suggestions on befriending internationals, especially students and refugees:

- Work with the foreign student office on your local college campus to welcome international students. Meet arriving students at the airport, and make sure they have housing for the first few nights. The U.S. Citizenship and Immigration Services can provide guidelines for refugees (uscis.gov).
- Help internationals find permanent housing and get settled. Show them how to read classified ads.
- Take them on orientation visits to local stores, and show them how to shop.
- Orient them to the laws and street signs. Provide them with city maps and bus schedules.
- Invite them home for meals, or include them in other social activities. Remember to be sensitive to religious dietary restrictions and to moral codes, especially regarding men and women together.

- Sponsor or attend activities specifically for internationals. Churches sometimes organize picnics, retreats, sporting events, sightseeing tours, or trips to museums or zoos to build friendships with internationals.
- Encourage those interested in learning about Christianity to attend church services or a church social event. Use the holidays of Thanksgiving, Christmas, and Easter to explain the Christian faith.
- Hold a one-day conference at your church on the Christian faith, using seminars on the Bible and Christian living—integrated with lots of hospitality—to introduce internationals to the basics of faith.[6]

Principles for Outreach: Learning

Finally, *be a learner*. Learning about the country from which our international friends have come and greeting them in their native language express a deep interest in the people we are trying to befriend. If we want them to listen to us talk about Christianity, we reciprocate by listening to their views without condemnation or ridicule.

Joking about sacred cows with Hindus, laughing at fanatical Muslims, or demeaning the intensity of Roman Catholicism in Latin America or the Philippines is no way to show respect to our international friends. Because we, as Christians, believe in the value of every person, our lives should reflect respect for and a desire to understand our foreign friends.

Once again, outreach is our greatest reason for gathering information about our world. One international student from Cape Verde became my friend instantly, simply because I knew where he lived and that he spoke Portuguese. A taxi driver in Atlanta almost drove off the road with excitement because I knew the names of three cities in his home country of Nigeria. Workers I meet from Ethiopia immediately light up when I greet them in their mother tongue of Amharic. If internationals sense that we have a genuine interest in learning about their homes, they are usually very willing to interact with us.

One final thought about learning: Some Americans grow impatient with internationals when they cannot understand the accents or the broken English. Learning implies patience. Ask international friends to speak slowly, and then do the same for them. (Remember to speak slower, not louder; internationals are not deaf; they are simply learning English.) The more internationals we befriend, the better we decipher accents, pronunciations, and sentence structure.

The Impact

Ministering to international students usually means touching the lives of the future leaders of business, government, and education. The former king of Nepal, the aforementioned prime minister of Pakistan, and dozens of international leaders of business and government were educated in the United States. Will we take the time to befriend their successors studying at the university in a nearby city? If we, in the past, had reached out to international students in the Boston area, perhaps the course of entire nations could have been changed.

Mark Rente, while a professor at Arizona State University, wrote about his impact on national leaders:

> Last year after we invited my foreign students to dinner, my wife and I were astonished to learn that we were in all likelihood breaking bread with future leaders. One of my students, Khaled, in replying to another student's question, mentioned that his father had been president for five years.
>
> "Of what company?" I asked.
>
> "Of my country," he replied.

His wife nodded adding, "President Abdullah al-Sallal, Khaled's father, is commonly referred to as having given birth to North Yemen."[7]

A couple who taught in Oman, a devoutly Muslim nation on the Saudi Arabian Peninsula, told me that the sultan of Oman is very favorable toward Christians in his country. To accommodate foreign workers, he contributed land for building churches. The sultan's unusual benevolence toward Christians stems from his experiences as a foreign student in England. When he studied there, a British Christian took him into his home and befriended him. That anonymous man's outreach now affects an entire Muslim nation.

Evangelizing those who are not reachable through conventional missions is another impact of reaching out to internationals. Christie, my wife, has an ongoing ministry to a lab technologist from India, whom she befriended as she trained him in parasitology. In the process, she touched a devout Hindu who, until then, had only misconceptions about Christianity. His daughter now attends a Catholic school, and Christie's co-worker brings his questions about Christianity to work so Christie can explain Christian beliefs to him.

A friend works with Chinese scholars who come to study at the Massachusetts Institute of Technology (MIT). One scholar studying this year is from the Uygur ethnic minority, one of the official "hidden people groups" listed by the U.S. Center for World Mission. If this man learns of and responds to Jesus, he may be God's agent for taking the gospel to an ethnic group that presently has no knowledge of Jesus Christ.

When a job opportunity working in Saudi Arabia came his way, a businessman with a deep conviction about reaching Muslims for Christ came to talk with me. He hoped that such an assignment could put him as an evangelist near Islam's holiest city, Mecca. Further research, however, revealed that his job assignment would put him on an American compound with little opportunity to meet Saudis. As he prayed about the opportunity, God led him to get involved in international student ministry in Boston, where there were many from Saudi Arabia whom he could befriend and evangelize freely.

Another impact of ministry with internationals relates to training cross-cultural workers who will go from the United States to other countries. The couple who taught in Oman prepared before they went by getting involved with Arabic-speaking people here in Boston. As a result of their ministry here in Boston, they spoke Arabic fluently, and they had a team of Arabic-speaking Christians in Boston praying for them as they served in Oman.

While Tom and Victoria prepared to plant churches in Rio de Janeiro, Brazil, they attended a Brazilian Pentecostal church close to their home. When they returned to the United States, Tom thrilled that church by preaching in Portuguese about their work in Rio. In turn, the church shared with Tom and Victoria about their ministry to the Brazilian community (more than fifty thousand) in the Boston area.

Internationals can help train cross-cultural workers for the culture, language, and traditions of the countries to which they go. This reciprocal ministry uniquely reflects the theme of the Lausanne Congress for World Evangelization: "The whole church takes the whole Gospel to the whole world."

Three World-Class Stories

Story 1: The Gospel and the Princess of Bhutan

Several years ago, I spent some time learning about and praying for the mysterious and virtually unreachable country of Bhutan. Located in the Himalayan region of Asia, Bhutan stays locked in Tibetan-style Buddhism and removed from the modern world. Around the same time, my friends, a husband and wife serving as dorm parents at a nearby university, invited Christie and me to dinner.

When we arrived, the husband said, "Before we eat, we have a surprise for you." They took us into the university's dining hall to introduce us to a young international student—from Bhutan! Later, our friends told us, "That young woman is the favorite daughter of the favorite wife of the king of Bhutan. We thought you'd like to meet someone who might be the answer to your prayers for this country." Indeed, if the princess of Bhutan responds to the gospel she learned of from our friends and from Christian students, an entire nation could be changed.

Story 2: "I Am Miao!"

I stood in the hallway of a Pennsylvania church, preparing to speak at a dinner held by the church every September to welcome international students attending the local university. The church had "adopted" as their global prayer focus the Miao people of south China, an ethnic group with little exposure to the gospel. Posters throughout the church displayed pictures, statistics, and prayer requests for these people. And in bold print, each poster read, PRAY FOR THE MIAO.

As I stood in the hallway, a young man asked me, "Are you from this church?" His accent gave away that he was an international student, and I assumed from his face that he was from China.

"No," I replied. "I'm a visitor. This is my first time in this church."

"Me too," he said. "This is my first time visiting *any* church. I'm a first-year graduate student from China."

Then, pointing to the PRAY FOR THE MIAO poster, he asked, "Do you know what this is?"

I tried to explain the church's desire that every person have a chance to respond to God's love through Jesus, including this ethnic group in south China that had little knowledge of Jesus. And I told the young man of the church's commitment to pray for this group and, perhaps, to someday send Christian workers to that region of China.

His face brightened, and he said, "It is most amazing! *I am Miao.*"

That church had started praying for the Miao people half a world away. They were reaching out to international students in their midst. And at that moment God brought both outreaches together—the people they were praying for had come to them in the person of this young graduate student.

Story 3: Muammar al-Gaddafi's First Christian Prayer

Nate Mirza, a first-generation American, has dedicated his life to reaching out to internationals living in the United States. In his *Enabler* newsletter, Mirza recounted the following story from the mid-1980s. It remains perhaps the most amazing contemporary account of God working through a Christian committed to befriending an international.

> In 1986, an Englishman, Graham Lacey, and some friends were in New York. They asked themselves who would be the loneliest man in New York City. Concluding it was the Libyan ambassador, they invited him to Thanksgiving dinner. He surprised them by showing up and said, "If people knew who I am, they would spit in my face. Your country has just bombed mine. Your people don't like Colonel [Gaddafi], my leader."
>
> After several weeks of interaction with him, Lacey received an invitation from [Gaddafi] to visit Libya in August 1987. During an audience with the leader in his Bedouin tent, Lacey was accused of believing a Zionist lie. He answered, "Sir, I know Jesus Christ personally. I've experienced him in my life."

After more than an hour's discussion, Lacey asked to pray with [Gaddafi]. Following discussion with his advisers, the Colonel looked him straight in the face and said, "Sir, you may pray."

"I prayed in the name of our Lord and Savior," Lacey said, "for [Gaddafi's] salvation, for his wife's and his family's and for revival, for an unprecedented outpouring of the Holy Spirit's power in Libya."

[Gaddafi] embraced him and after more discussion with his advisers in Arabic, Lacey was told, "The distinguished leader would like you to pray again." As Lacey hesitated, [Gaddafi] told him, "Nobody has ever told me before about Jesus. Nobody but a Muslim has ever prayed with me. I would like you to get down on your knees and pray again. This time Libyan television will televise it."[8]

Biblical Texts to Study

• Exodus 22:21

• Leviticus 19:33–34

• Deuteronomy 10:17–19; 16:10–14

• Psalm 96

• Hebrews 13:1–2

Things to Talk About

• Have you ever been "the foreigner" in a situation? What adjustments, problems, or fears did you face? How did you face them?

• Referencing the Scriptures above, what actions and considerations should we show to "foreigners" (CEV)? What attitudes are prescribed in these passages?

• Read Luke 10:25–37. What are some of the costs of helping our international neighbor?

• Read Acts 8:26–40. What resulted from Philip's faithful witness to this international?

• What are some specific ways we can reach out to internationals in our area?

GOING GLOBAL

To live life to the fullest, you have to experience the world.
HENRY STANLEY

The bumper sticker caught my eye: THINK GLOBALLY, ACT LOCALLY. The theme rings true for all who aspire to grow as a world-class Christian. God calls us to think (and pray, give, understand, and live) with a *global* perspective and to act *locally* to affect lives around us for the advancement of his kingdom. Bob Roberts Jr. calls this *Glocalization.*[1]

Local involvement often comes first, but God also thrusts us outward. We desire to grow in our understanding of God's world, so we go beyond our normal comfort zones into involvement with other people from other cultures and (if possible) in other parts of the world.

Going global introduces us to risks. It's risky to try to relate to someone from a culture different from our own. It's risky to travel overseas to places where standards of hygiene are different from those we might be accustomed to. It's a challenge to try to communicate with someone who doesn't speak our language.

Risk goes hand in hand with adventure. As we step out and take risks, we trust God in new ways, which deepens our faith and makes our Christian commitment come to life. Paul Tournier, the great Swiss psychologist, writes:

> Throughout the history of the church, it has been this reversal in attitude [the desire for security and a risk-free environment] that has raised up martyrs and the heroes of the faith, has given them their indomitable strength, their complete independence as regards men and events, even at the times of greatest failure. . . . What matters is to listen to [God], to let ourselves be guided, to face up to the adventure to which he calls us, with all its risks. Life is an adventure directed by God.[2]

Low-Risk Starters

Paratroopers do not start their training by jumping out of a plane; they start by jumping off platforms, getting accustomed to the pull of opening parachutes, and addressing from the ground their fear of heights. Going global does not start with getting on a jet for the first time and leaving for the remote jungles of Papua New Guinea. But it might start by corresponding with a worker from Wycliffe Bible Translators or New Tribes Mission in Papua New Guinea.

We can feel free to start small. Taking the risk of going out to eat international food might be all we can take. Eating hot salsa at the Mexican restaurant might be a risk for us, but let's do it! Rationalizing—"Since I'm not headed overseas, I need not have an interest in any place other than my home culture"—misses the opportunity to learn in our ever-shrinking global village.

Over the years, I've gathered many low-risk starters—ideas to help individuals and families get started building a world-class home environment. Here are a few:

- Host a worker returning from another country, giving your family the chance to hear about life in a foreign culture. Help your children see that people actually live in the countries they see on a map.

- Call or write to people serving as missionaries, or correspond with foreign friends. Bring the world "over there" into your home, mail, or email box.

- Handle something from another country. Of all the influences that prompted me to think about the world, the earliest I can remember was my interest in foreign coins and stamps on letters from international friends. Looking at these introduced me, as a child, to the fascinating reality that "our world" is not the only world.

- Host for dinner an international student or a friend from another culture, or house an exchange student for a year. Help your children know people of a different culture, skin color, and language.

- Attend cultural events in neighborhoods ethnically different from your own. Or regularly eat out together at an international restaurant. Develop an appreciation for other traditions and foods.

- Keep a stack of prayer cards at the dinner table or a map nearby to pray for one country or international worker at every family meal.

- Support as a family an international project or a child overseas.

- Learn about the countries on the "Made in" labels of your clothing. One homeschooling mom built geography lessons on the twenty-six nations recorded on her sons' clothing labels. And pray for the textile worker who assembled your clothing: the Muslim from "Made in Bangladesh" and the Buddhist from "Made in Cambodia," all people who need to know about Jesus.

- Take a vacation with a purpose (within the United States) to help at a mission agency headquarters or to help with a vacation Bible school in a church ethnically different from your own.

An article in *Moody Monthly* instructed readers on "How to Be a Foreign Missionary . . . Without Leaving Home."[3] Through prayer, correspondence, and a personal strategy, the author demonstrated how we could serve overseas by being partners with international workers—even if we never go ourselves. Technology, the Internet, and mass communications make the suggestions in that article easy.

Going global with even these small risks opens a new world of growth for our world-class families.

Medium-Range Risks

After we grow accustomed to the international outreach we can have from our home base, we can venture out a little farther. Now the risks and the investments require greater commitments.

The Stevens family read these prophetic words in an article by Tom Sine: "The United States and Western Europe of the nineties will continue to become more ethnically diverse. . . . Young people raised in the all-white suburbs of America and able to converse in only one language will become the culturally disadvantaged of the nineties. They will be ill-equipped to participate in the increasingly cross-cultural and transnational environment of tomorrow's world."[4]

Not wanting their children or themselves to be "culturally disadvantaged," Mr. and Mrs. Stevens enrolled in an evening Spanish course at a community college, and they encouraged their children to take Spanish in school. The family members went on to commit themselves to serve twice a year in a Hispanic neighborhood in the city, and they try to worship four times a year at a Spanish-speaking congregation in order to improve their language fluency and to broaden their understanding of the global Christian church. Language learning is time consuming, humiliating, and sometimes frustrating, but it's also a commitment to expand our cultural diversity in the internationalized world in which we live.

For the people at our home church (growing in its ethnic diversity but still a predominantly white, middle-class, suburban church), medium-range risks include service ventures into the city. Dr. John Perkins, founder of the Harambee Christian Center in Los Angeles, exhorts Christians against the "dangers of a homogeneous fellowship." He encourages everyone to have Christian brothers and sisters from many racial and ethnic backgrounds. He observes that "belonging to a group whose members are like oneself requires no faith. . . . Reconciling bigots is a far greater sign of the supernatural than is speaking in tongues."[5]

When teenager Margie Hanson entered her first heterogeneous fellowship, she was serving in an ethnically diverse neighborhood in a poor part of Newark, New Jersey. Her experiences were published in a national youth magazine as an example for other young people:

> Margie's job in Newark (New Jersey) was to help in a day-care center with first- and second-graders. "When I first walked into the room and saw all these little black kids, I thought, I'll never be able to tell them apart"—a stereotype she didn't even know she held.
>
> But within a day, she could not only tell them apart, she had fallen in love with them. . . . Margie went to Newark expecting to give, to help. Instead, she says, she was mostly on the receiving end, and she learned a lot about giving. Margie and the five others on the trip lived with several single mothers in government housing. . . . "They gave up their bedrooms for us. It was very hot that week and they gave us the only fan. They would get up early and make us an incredible breakfast

every morning. They'd always wait up for us at night and do other little things, like put a Hershey's kiss on our pillows."

Those two weeks in the inner city—two weeks in which she was the minority, the only white face in a sea of black faces—changed Margie. She realized that while she can walk away from the reality of interracial tensions after two weeks in the inner city—because she is white—many people can't. She determined to make a difference where she could.[6]

Margie's cross-cultural experience in the city changed her life and worldview. She went to college determined to work in the city, and after graduation, she served at an orphanage in Calcutta, India. Her great influence now is as a mom challenging her family and church to be actively involved in cross-cultural friendships, racial reconciliation, and personal outreach to those "different" from themselves.

Going global might not involve international travel. For Carol, it means a weekly trip to a homeless shelter to deliver meals that she and other homemakers have prepared. For Karl and Karen, it means leading a youth group, the sons and daughters of Cambodian refugees. For Ben, it means offering his painting services to inner-city ministries.

One other idea is to consider those who are physically or mentally challenged. Although these people are usually not from a different culture in the usual sense, they do have a subculture of their own that needs to be penetrated with the love of Christ. And yet, the risks we take are real; we will feel awkward at first to work with the chronically ill, the hearing-impaired, the blind, or the mentally ill. But just as Margie Hanson grew through her service in the inner city, so we are required to trust God when we serve those with disabilities.

Medium-range risks take us into the world where people from other cultures and races actually live so that we might, in a small way, identify with them and their worlds. Following the example of Jesus (John 1:14), involvement sends us out to incarnate his love.

Higher and Wider Risks

A travel agency near Harvard University advertised travel with three words: "Please . . . Go Away." In the world of Adoniram Judson, the first white missionary sent from the shores of North America, global travel for the average person was out of the question. It took three months to sail from the East Coast of the United States to India. Today, however, we can travel from New York City to India in less than two days.

Several years ago, I flew from my home airport in Boston to California (to speak at a Sunday morning church service). On Sunday afternoon, I flew from California to Singapore to Kathmandu, Nepal (arriving Tuesday morning for a youth conference held Tuesday through Friday). Friday evening I flew back through Singapore to California (arriving Saturday to speak at another Sunday morning church service). Then I flew home to Boston (arriving on the "red-eye" flight Monday morning). Crazy? Yes. But traveling into other countries and experiencing other cultures is open to us as never before.

Edie Irish of Flint, Michigan, illustrates the world of travel open to us. As a member of the Traveler's Century Club (reserved for those who have visited one hundred or more foreign countries), this grandmother has now set foot in 293 of the world's 308 nations and island groups. By making travel her priority, she opened herself to all manner of exploration and risk, including trips to Libya, Angola, and Chad.[7]

Bob expands his view of the Christian church around the world by extending his international business trips. His position takes him overseas four times per year, and he uses free time and weekends to visit national churches, encourage international workers, and learn about the stresses of cross-cultural adaptation. His growth comes with a risk, because it means leaving the security of Americanized compounds or conference centers to get out on the streets of Hong Kong, Bogotá, or Nairobi. But by making advance contact with missionaries or local believers, he is escorted by people who know the language and the culture.

Hank is a single man who spends his leisure time on cross-cultural trips. He leads short-term service teams from his church almost every year. Sometimes he simply travels with "adventure travel" groups in an effort to grow in his world vision. These vacations-with-a-purpose have resulted in Hank's service on the global-outreach committee and in his increased financial commitments to international projects.

Short-term mission efforts, once reserved for collegians, are now available to adults of all ages. They give us the chance to visit overseas workers our churches support, see the work of the gospel in another country, meet Christian sisters and brothers overseas, and grow in our understanding of the world. Consider some examples:

- My widowed mother traveled to Kenya (East Africa) on her first-ever mission trip/vacation—at age sixty-seven. She was willing to take the risk because a seventy-year-old friend challenged her to join in the expedition!

- Saddleback Church and Willow Creek Community Church, regarded as the largest evangelical churches in America, have sent thousands of cross-cultural team participants to learn and serve. Why? Because "we feel that one way to educate our people to God's worldwide program is through hands-on involvement. So short-term ministries into Mexico, even to the inner city of Chicago and elsewhere, form a primary emphasis in our ministry."[8]

- In our home church of Grace Chapel, over one hundred youth and adults participate annually in short-term mission service in other cultures. By returning to the same locations, church members feel a special partner-ship with ministries in Moldova, Malawi, Trinidad, and Egypt.

Short-term service opportunities should not be some sort of affluent voyeurism, what one person critiqued as "poor tours." Instead, they offer involvement: "Get dusty. Stay for two nights with a Mexican family. Learn what the tourists never learn."[9] The higher risks of short-term mission travel are worth it, because they offer growth and service opportunities that allow us to live alongside brothers and sisters from every tribe, tongue, and nation, giving us that "preview of heaven" referred to earlier.

Look for These Results

Going global is not merely an excuse for collecting experiences or accumulating new stamps in our passports. Our reason for cross-cultural involvement is to grow as world-class Christians. We go out so that we can grow as people whose lifestyles and obedience are increasingly compatible, that is, in cooperation and in accord with what God wants to do in our world through us.

Significant Personal Growth

When we start taking these low, medium, and high risks, we can look for *significant personal growth*. His travels across Africa in search of Dr. David Livingstone caused Henry Stanley to write, "To live life to the fullest, you have to experience the world." His experiences in other cultures widened his understanding of life itself. Even secular college organizations realize that personal growth comes from self-less service. For example, a program designed to use students' energy for service (keeping them away from the raucous parties of spring break) advertised itself this way: "Instead of Beer, Volunteer."

On the Christian front, single-adult ministry specialist Chris Eaton writes, "Everybody says they go to serve and give, and every year they come back saying, 'I couldn't give enough compared to what the people gave me. What I learned far outweighs what I taught.'"[10] A student returned from a summer of cross-cultural service and wrote, "God taught me I was never alone. He was with me always. And every time that I was weak, he was strong. Every single time! He would always seem to turn my particular weakness into his strength, and that was amazing to see."[11]

On my personal trips overseas and into other cultures in the United States, I've noticed that I pray more, consciously trust God more, and grow more. Fully aware that my life is out of my control, I trust it to God—and my faith comes to life in a new way.

An Enlarged Perspective

When we go global, we can also look for an *enlarged perspective*. My injury on the basketball court led to surgery and three months in a cast. Although I struggled with the normal self-pity that accompanies any such inconvenience, I realized how overseas travel had changed my perspective. I could not complain. I had a clean hospital, expert surgeons, and physical therapy to speed my recovery. A man I met in Angola, about my age, suffered an injury similar to mine, which left him crippled for life.

We do not go overseas or into new cultures to exert some sort of expertise we found through reading travel books. We go as servants and as learners. We go, asking God to change our perspectives— opening ourselves to whatever changes he wants to make in us through what we see and experience. I explain, when training college and graduate school students for a short-term mission effort, that one purpose of our service is to understand that U.S. culture is not the standard by which all others are measured. We want them to be open to a change in perspective.

Dale Hanson Bourke, author and former editor of *Today's Christian Woman,* wrote of her change in perspective because of a trip into another culture:

> I had just returned from a trip to Latin America, and the shock of reentry into American society was fresh. Everywhere I turned, I was amazed by our abundance of things. In the grocery superstore, for example, I stared at the produce department for several minutes, suppressing my desire to gather up the shiny red apples . . . and send them to the children I had seen begging on the streets of Guatemala City just a few days before. I looked at the rack of reduced items and realized that the people I had seen living on the city dump would find the overripe fruit and dented cans to be unimaginable treasures.[12]

She goes on to describe her perspectives on contrasts. With the poor in the barrios of Latin America, she saw a love for children and the wealth of sharing. With the rich in that U.S. superstore, she saw children abused and people living with dulled moral sensitivities. "I had seen wealth in spirit amidst poverty, and now I saw poverty disguised by wealth."[13]

Increased Witnessing

When we go global, we can look for an *increase in our witness.* Those who spend vacation time with the Christian Medical Society's medical caravans in Honduras get to share their experiences with peers. This sharing usually leads to an explanation of why they serve others overseas.

Our friends who spend one weekend per month serving in the inner city often have great opportunities to share their faith with co-workers at Monday's coffee break, when the discussion centers on "What did you do this weekend?" The outward expression of

Christian faith through cross-cultural serving gives credibility to our commitment, and people stand up and notice.

Christie and I have noticed that our overseas service gives us the opportunity to share at home with our friends who've never heard the gospel. After our trips to places such as Colombia or Sri Lanka or Burundi, they ask, "Why would you want to go there?" Our answers give us the chance to explain what it means to be given over to the lordship of Jesus Christ.

Indiana Jones for Jesus

The young boys in the Christian Service Brigade braced themselves for another boring speaker. It was "missions night," and some feared the worse. To their surprise, the speaker started by asking, "How would you like to be an Indiana Jones for Jesus?"

The boys started to perk up, thinking, *Let's hear more about this.*

"What is it that attracts us to the exploits of Indiana Jones?" the speaker asked.

Boys raised their hands and fired out ideas:

"He lives a life of adventure."

"He goes to exotic places."

"He eats weird things."

"He hangs around with interesting people."

"He confronts evil powers."

"He seeks after and finds treasures."

"He lives on the edge of danger."

Then the speaker, an international mission agency executive, described how the worldwide call of God needs young people who are willing to be an Indiana Jones for Jesus. He explained with stories about the need for men and women who would go out and take risks—even the risk of dying—to spread the gospel. These adventurers for Jesus might go to places our world thinks are exotic—such as Bombay, Kathmandu, Santiago, or Moscow—to tell people about the Lord. Strange foods, fascinating people, exposure to the powers of Satan, and guaranteed danger lie ahead for those who follow God's call into other cultures. But they would persevere like Indiana Jones, because they were after the greatest treasure of all: the treasure of seeing others come to know Jesus Christ.

The boys generally agreed that the mission speaker "wasn't as boring as we'd expected," and they went home dreaming of the risks that Jesus might call them to take.

If, as Tournier says, "Life is an adventure directed by God," we face the challenge of being adventurers for Jesus. Will you step out and go global (even if it's only short term) in an effort to understand and be more aware of our world? Taking such a risk will change your life.

Biblical Texts to Study

- Acts 16

- 2 Corinthians 11:16–33

Things to Talk About

- Referencing the Scriptures above, identify some of the risks—low, medium, or high—taken by the apostle Paul in spreading the gospel.

- What attitudes, motives, and strengths were behind Paul's risk taking?

- What positive and negative results occurred from the risks Paul took?

- What results might we expect from taking risks in cross-cultural outreach?

- Identify one practical and appropriate low-risk action you will take in cross-cultural outreach. What medium-risk action will you take? What global, high-risk goal will you work toward?

11

NEARSIGHTEDNESS

The light that shines farthest shines the brightest close to home.
OSWALD J. SMITH

One community church has a tremendous global vision. A huge map in the foyer highlights their international partners (both missionaries and national leaders) serving in over one hundred countries. Flags hanging in the sanctuary represent some of these countries. A thermometer off to one side shows their progress in funding the year's global outreach budget of $2 million. Each year, for the past seventy years, the church has given to international missions more than they gave the previous year!

A visitor to this church immediately notices their commitment to the worldwide advance of the gospel; but after a few months, discerning worshipers begin to notice the conspicuous lack of concern for the local area. Millions of dollars are raised for foreign endeavors, but there is little emphasis on reaching out to their community and nearby city.

One insightful staff member critiqued the community church this way: "We are great on farsightedness, looking out for the needs of 'the world'; but we are almost blind to nearsighted issues. I fear sometimes that we excuse our personal responsibility to witness by highlighting our overseas involvement, and, in so doing, we may help evangelize people half a world away while our neighbors die without knowledge of Christ."

This church's problems are not unique. Any church that takes on the challenge of producing world-class Christians can get so involved in the drastic needs of other places and cultures that they overlook the needs next door. Like the religious leaders in the parable of the good Samaritan, we risk using our concern for world needs as an excuse to step over broken persons at our feet, near our doorstep, or in our neighborhood.

Oswald J. Smith, mission catalyst and founder of the Peoples Church in Toronto, exhorted his people to stay balanced between global service and local service. He observed that "the light that shines the farthest shines the brightest close to home." He delighted himself in the global outreach of his church, but he knew that worldwide giving and missions conferences did not replace the need for outreach right in the community.

The world-class Christian grows by investigating, "God, what do you want me to do—starting right here at home?"

You Shall Be My Witnesses

At our church, the Cross-Cultural Training Program trains people for future assignments in other cultures. One week, we met intending to study methods of cross-cultural evangelism. But as we gathered, I suddenly realized that I was not sure we could communicate the gospel to people in our secular, considerably unchurched Boston suburb.

We deferred the lecture on methods of cross-cultural evangelism to the next meeting and instead spent the evening learning to share the gospel in a concise way, using Campus Crusade's booklet *The Four Spiritual Laws*. I explained that although the booklet was not a perfect tool, God could use it to help us get the gospel message across.

Then came our assignment. Each of us was to share *The Four Spiritual Laws* (or some other gospel-presentation tool) with one person before the next meeting. One young man, who still had not grasped the need for "nearsighted" concern, raised his hand and asked, "But what if I don't meet anyone from another culture in that time?" I explained that he should look for friends, relatives, or co-workers with whom he had never directly discussed the gospel. His outreach in these cases did not need to be cross-cultural.

Two weeks later, we met again and reported our gospel-sharing experiences. Some had been unsuccessful; no one would talk with them about the gospel. Others had gone through the booklet but felt awkward, since it was the first time they had explained the gospel. A few had failed with the booklet but succeeded in gospel-oriented discussions with their co-workers.

The most dramatic story came from Fran. Almost two weeks had passed before she remembered the assignment, and she needed someone to talk to. The only person available was her aging father. Fran went through *The Four Spiritual Laws* with her dad, and at the close of the presentation, he prayed to commit himself to Jesus Christ. Fran was excited because she had never before talked with her father about knowing Jesus Christ personally and preparing for eternity.

Here was Fran—a potential international worker preparing for cross-cultural service as a missionary—witnessing to her father for the first time! The experience reminded me of Jesus' commission to be his witnesses in Jerusalem first (Acts 1:8). Imagine what it meant for the disciples to be witnesses in front of their friends, perhaps their families, and their countrymen—to speak boldly for Jesus before people who had seen them fail, deny Christ several weeks earlier, and then run into hiding.

We identify with those disciples, because being a witness to people we know is especially difficult. In some respects, it might have been easier for Fran to evangelize someone in a foreign land or in another culture—someone she might never see again—than to be Jesus' witness to her father, whom she had known all her life. The same might be true for us if we share the gospel with any relative, longtime neighbor, or co-worker who knows well our sins and failures.

A world-class Christian, however, is committed to outreach and evangelism both at home and around the world. For many of us, the people we affect most are in our own culture and neighborhood, so our commitment calls us to witness to them.

One motivation for witness is the spiritually lost condition of people who don't acknowledge Jesus Christ as Savior (John 3:36). But we must remember—as we study about "hidden people" who have no way of knowing Jesus or about millions of Muslims, Hindus, and Buddhists without Christ—lostness is a spiritual state, not a geographic state.

In other words, my neighbor who worships financial success and my friends who live with no belief in eternity are just as lost as any person bowing down to the golden Buddha. A Buddhist in Thailand may appear more lost to me than my friend down the street, but from a biblical perspective, they both desperately need Jesus. And, at this time in my life, I can pray for the Buddhist, but I am in a position to present Christ to my neighbors and friends.

Interest in and commitment to world-class Christian outreach and evangelism begin right where we live. We cannot excuse witness in our community by an excessive interest in people beyond the reach of our personal evangelism.

Space does not allow for a detailed explanation on the how-tos of witnessing. But the following are excellent resources on this topic (see also Resources for Further Growth).

- *Stop Witnessing . . . and Start Loving* by Paul Borthwick offers practical ideas to build our impact as local witnesses for Jesus.
- *How to Reach Secular People* by George G. Hunter helps us gain spiritual insight in secular settings.
- *Becoming a Contagious Christian* by Bill Hybels and Mark Mittelburg and *Becoming a Contagious Church* by Mark Mittelburg are evangelism classics. (Available as a seminar and in many media formats.)
- *Divine Appointments* by Jacks, Jacks, and Mellskog inspires us to see every interpersonal encounter as an opportunity from God.
- *Out of the Saltshaker and into the World* by Rebecca Manley Pippert inspires and offers practical tools on evangelism as a lifestyle.
- *The Great Omission* by J. Robertson McQuilkin challenges us to evaluate if we believe lost people really are lost.
- *Foolishness to the Greeks* and *The Gospel in a Pluralistic Society* by Lesslie Newbigin inspire us to see our own culture with missionary eyes.
- *Evangelism Outside the Box* by Rick Richardson focuses on telling the "old, old story" in new ways to a postmodern generation.
- *The Case for Christ* by Lee Strobel is an apologetic resource evidencing the life of Christ.

You Shall Be My Catalysts

Nearsightedness—paying attention to the needs around us—obviously starts with an active outreach to those near us who don't know Jesus. But nearsightedness also means looking for ways to affect our churches with a world-class Christian vision.

Dick wanted to go into cross-cultural ministry as a tentmaker in a Muslim country. When I served my church as minister of missions, Dick and I were catching up on the events of the past few months since he graduated from college. I asked what I thought was a fair question: "Dick, if you desire to go overseas as one of our missionaries, why haven't you been involved in some aspect of our local church ministry?"

I expected comments about his being newly graduated or not knowing where to help or being too busy. Instead, I heard something else.

"Well," Dick replied, his eyes widening as he got agitated, "this church—all churches that I know of—doesn't really care about the Great Commission. All I see are self-centered people, preoccupied with their own pet peeves—service times, whether child care is offered, and improvements to the physical plant—and little interest in winning the world for Christ."

Dick's countenance changed from anger to shame. He had spoken his mind, but he realized that he was talking to a member of the pastoral staff, who represented both the "self-centered" people of the congregation and the funding that he needed to go out in service. I think he expected me to defend my case.

Instead, I simply replied, "Dick, some of your observations are true, although I think you have overlooked many fine people and churches. But this is exactly why I asked for your involvement. We need people like you to be catalysts toward greater missions involvement while you are here. You see, Dick, whether we like to admit it or not, the local church is primary in God's worldwide purposes."

I then pointed out to him four essential truths about the local church, truths that could help him change his perspective and become a catalyst for the growth of world-class Christians in our fellowship.

Truth 1: The Local Church Is Primary in World Missions Because Jesus Said It Is

The promise of Jesus to Peter (Matthew 16:18) states that he will build his church and the gates of hell will not prevail against it. The image is of a forceful organization of believers representing one kingdom on the march against another. When the gates of that kingdom—hell—are attacked, they will fall because of God's power working through his church.

Who is supposed to be on this attack? Jesus says it's his church. For each of us, this manifests itself in the local assembly of believers. The church fails in its task when it loses the mentality of advancement.

The local church that is a foe to world missions or a failure in doing its part in the Great Commission has usually degenerated from being a "kingdom advancer" to being a "fortress builder." Rather than taking new ground for Christ, we spend our time protecting the turf we have.

Truth 2: The Local Church Is Primary in World Missions Because the Body of Christ Is There

Peer groups and campus fellowships can be wonderful stimuli toward discipleship and worldwide involvement, but they do not represent the whole cross section of the body of Christ. The local church offers the broadest range of spiritual gifts, a range that usually cannot be found in small-group fellowships.

Truth 3: The Local Church Is Primary in World Missions Because It Affords Us Training and Care

I asked Dick, "Do you have the patience needed to persevere for years in a Muslim culture without seeing anyone become a Christian?" Then I answered for him, "No one really knows. But ministry to the junior highers at the local church can certainly help develop patience. And do you desire to lead people in another culture to Christ, disciple them, and encourage them to be world-class Christians? If you do, you have every opportunity to test skills, methods, and relational abilities right in your own church."

Truth 4: The Local Church Is Primary in World Missions Because It Both Begins and Ends Our Global, Cross-Cultural Outreach

In his book *A People for His Name*, Dr. Paul A. Beals identifies in the Book of Acts a three-part cycle regarding the outreach effort of the early Christians:

1. Evangelizing nonbelievers
2. Edifying the saints
3. Establishing churches[1]

As soon as a new church was established, the cycle resumed: evangelizing—edifying—establishing. The problem of the established church is that we perceive ourselves as being the end of the cycle, not the beginning of a new one (the fortress mentality).

I concluded by asking Dick to work with us as a catalyst to make the local church a gathering of world-class Christians.

How to Be a Catalyst

The intensity of a fire is measured not only by the heat it gives off but also by the number of nearby objects it ignites. If we desire to affect our local churches with a global, world-class Christian vision, the place to start is with our own "fire." The best way to get others burning with a vision for prayer, lifestyle change, and outreach—both locally and worldwide—is to be on fire ourselves. As we grow in intensity, those around us will be ignited.

Beyond our personal example, however, applying some basic principles will help us be catalysts for a world-class vision in our local churches.[2]

Principle: Make Missions Manageable

People come to church for a variety of reasons. Some come to satisfy a genuine spiritual hunger. Others come to meet social as well as spiritual needs. Children and young people may come at the will of their parents. Hurting people come to be cared for. The motivations vary widely, although spiritual growth is at least one of the driving forces.

It's safe to assume, however, that most do not come to church to get overwhelmed by statistics, needs, and guilt-producing overviews of the task of worldwide outreach. The needs related to health, hunger, and poverty are greater than ever, and the inequities between the rich and the poor of our world are overwhelming. Of the almost 7 billion people on earth

- 2.2 billion have no access to safe drinking water;
- 2 billion live in poverty (under $2 a day); 1.1 billion of these live in extreme poverty (under $1 a day);
- 700 million dwell in shantytowns or slums;
- 700 million children are sick; each year, 30 million die from hunger (18 million of these are under age five);
- 120 million children live on the street.

And the statistics above, taken from the *World Christian Encyclopedia*, just scratch the surface. Urban sprawl exceeds the population of some countries; for example, some estimate that Mexico City's population is nearing 30 million, which exceeds the population of Canada or Australia. The long-term implications of HIV/AIDS to nations and the number of spiritually lost people in our country responding to non-Christian religions brought into the United States add up to one word: OVERLOAD!

A zealous woman who once attended our church tried to instill a global vision in others by quoting facts about needs and telling grim stories. With a propensity to induce guilt, she could quote so many statistics about world concerns that we nicknamed her "The Grim Heaper."

For most people in our churches—including me—the global perspective is too vast, too overwhelming. Therefore, painting pictures of millions or billions of people, thousands of "people groups," or hundreds of countries can be counterproductive in helping church members see their participation in world evangelization.

World Vision once printed a poster that summed up the need for a manageable response. A photo in the upper corner of the poster showed a mass of suffering humanity. The question that followed was, "How do you help 1 billion hungry people?" In the opposite, lower corner was a picture of one malnourished child. The caption? "One at a time."

One church supports a large number of outreach workers serving locally, in other parts of the United States, and in over twenty-five foreign countries. Even these facts overwhelm the average attender. But rather than encouraging everyone to get to know the entire family of workers, the outreach "catalysts" encourage people to adopt "just one"—one missionary family, one campus worker, or one global partner. To help interested members start a relationship with just one, they post information about their workers on the church's website, or they give Prayer Packets. These packets include recent newsletters, a photo, a one-page summary of the person's work, and a secure email address to get them started corresponding.

An attempt at one-at-a-time manageability in our church yielded a refrigerator magnet that said simply, "Do Something Once." The attached card gave people outreach ideas they could participate in just once: once a year (walk in the annual Walk for Hunger), once a month (write a letter to someone serving in another country), once a week (witness to a neighbor), and once a day (pray for someone who does not know Jesus). The "Do Something Once" campaign helps people move from the overwhelming world of more than 6 billion people to our personal worlds of one or two.

The following are other ideas to make global involvement meaningful, practical, and "one at a time" manageable:

- Encourage individuals, families, and small groups to adopt one "people group" for prayer and research (joshuaproject.net is most helpful).
- Focus on one international partner per month on the church website.
- Invite worship leaders to include one international prayer request per week in the worship services.
- Help others grow toward being world-class Christians by recommending to them simple starter books (see Resources for Further Growth for ideas).

It's far better to start small and build—including the whole church—than to overwhelm everyone to bear the vision alone. The best catalytic action is to help people understand missions in such a way that they can make a personal, manageable response.

Principle: Present the Global Cause Well

Several years ago, an international outreach committee requested and was granted time during the Sunday morning service to give a "World Focus" report through a DVD presentation. Believing they knew the world well, the committee members themselves produced the DVD, refusing the assistance of the worship department.

By the time the worship pastor previewed the DVD, there was no time left for editing. Recognizing the poor quality of the DVD, he said, "It was a poorly focused effort to focus our global efforts." The worship pastor was not nearsighted. In fact, he and his family went to the Middle East on a short-term mission trip. He simply was honest—the DVD *was* shabby.

Many of us have had similar experiences with global-focused presentations. The slide shows that stick in our minds are boring ones that foster stereotypes of pith helmets and out-of-date clothing—and they always close with the predictable sunset shot. Other presentations feature ill-prepared speakers whose gifts do not include preaching.

If we're to overcome the predictability, shabbiness, and poor performances of the past, we must make our presentations mindful that we "never get a second chance at a first impression." So, if we do finally get the opportunity to present a global-focused or international report in a major church service, let's do it well.

To help visitors who give international reports in your church service, consider producing an informational bulletin entitled *Presenting Well at Our Church*. In it, outline your church's constituency, your expectations of them as speakers, and how their presentation fits within the overall global plan of your church. Helpful instructions to share with your speakers might include the following:

- *Our church's culture of time.* "We're very time conscious, so please finish on time. We want people to leave saying, 'I wish I could hear more,' rather than 'I thought he would *never* stop.'"

- *The importance, or the unimportance, of attire.* "Ours is a formal, traditional church, so please wear a suit" or "Ours is a casual culture, so feel free to wear jeans (that is, do *not* wear a suit)." If people object and quote 1 Samuel 16:7, "Man looks at the outward appearance, but the LORD looks at the heart," remind them that both aspects are true; and since their presentation is primarily for people, we pay attention to the outward appearance. If needed, give presenters a cash allowance to purchase clothes that help them best fit in.

- *The importance of language.* "Over 50 percent of your listeners are new Christians, so please avoid overly religious language" or "Our church is very ethnically diverse; so please avoid cultural stereotypes."

- *Get help.* "We have people dedicated to helping you make the best use of technology (DVD, PowerPoint, and audio) for your presentation, so please ask for their help."

Sound harsh? Generally, guest speakers are grateful for the help, especially those making a cultural adjustment (or readjustment) to the United States. They appreciate the efforts to help them be culturally sensitive to the audience to whom they will speak.

Principle: Endure and Persist

Being a catalyst for a global vision in the local church is like swimming upstream—and it's often easier to quit and resort to floating along with popular opinion.

Global mission leaders, predicting the ability of the church to complete the Great Commission, list the local church as a major obstacle. Richard Sollis, former chair of the New Tribes Mission research-planning department, states, "By insufficient vision, discipleship, and obedience, the church has bottlenecked the flow of personnel and resources needed to do the job."[3] Jim Reapsome adds, "In a nutshell, apathetic Christians are the biggest hurdle to overcome."[4]

We need endurance to face *apathy.* Professor and former missionary Dr. J. Herbert Kane writes in his book *Wanted: World Christians!* "After the second or third generation, Christianity tends to take on cultural overtones, and soon its members begin to take their heritage for granted and lose all desire to share their faith with friends and neighbors. The churches turn inward on themselves, and soon their chief preoccupation is their own survivals, not the salvation of the world."[5]

We need endurance to face *all that distracts* our churches from an outward focus. A friend in ministry said to me in a letter, "We tried encouraging our church members to prioritize becoming world-class Christians. We were going to learn about other countries, expand our global outreach budget, and add some partners to our support list, but 'other things' waylaid us. A few crises in the church family, a church hassle over the Christmas program, and a staff resignation was all it took for our global plans to be tabled for another year. I simply do not know how to make the 'over there' proposition of world issues *real* to our people."

It's easy to give up. Genuine needs close to home deserve our attention, but we cannot let these needs diminish our overall commitment to see the gospel communicated to all people. Farsightedness must be balanced with nearsightedness.

Endurance is the willingness to persevere, even when there seems to be little *support.* Tom and Carolyn approached their church with a burden to see people involved in ministry to international students. At that time, only two or three families were interested. But Tom and Carolyn persevered. Three years later, their church hosted an annual Thanksgiving Conference for the International Students, Inc. (ISI) ministry. Over two hundred students attended, representing over forty countries. At that conference, almost seventy families from their church hosted students. Their endurance bore fruit.

Endurance is also the willingness to persevere, even when there seems to be little *interest.* In 1978, our church started sending young people on summer mission-service teams. At that time, only a few of our adults supported the idea. But endurance paid off. Now, an estimated three thousand young people, collegians, singles, and couples have gone out, totaling 150 service teams. Short-term mission-service teams have perhaps been the church's greatest asset for building excitement and commitment at the grass-roots level for cross-cultural outreach and involvement.

Brightening Our Corner

One of the Sunday school choruses of my childhood encouraged every Christian to "brighten the corner where you are." The idea in the song was that if every Christian would brighten his or her respective corner, more people could be introduced to Jesus.

The song highlights the need for world-class Christian nearsightedness. Investigating our role in God's worldwide commission commences with a look around us. Are there people we can touch with the love of Jesus? Is there a local church I can ignite with greater concern for outreach?

Concerns "over there" in international settings cannot be our solitary focus. If it is, we will cease to exercise the day-to-day love toward each other, which identifies us as the community of Christ. A commitment to missions should not imply a lopsided or one-sided view of ministry, but rather the nearsighted-farsighted balance.

Jack is committed to evangelism; as a layman, he leads his church's training program for evangelism. He is active as a Christian witness in his place of work, and he is solidly committed to world evangelization. He makes sure that his Sunday school class knows and prays for missionaries; he involves others by informing them about international outreach efforts. He uses his international business travel to learn more about God's work in other parts of the world. Jack has a growing "bifocal" vision, keeping a commitment to both "nearsighted" outreach and "farsighted" influence. Jack brightens his corner and acts as a catalyst for others to do the same.

Nearsightedness Test

Answer *yes* or *no* to each of the following statements; then score your test below.

_____ 1. I made a new acquaintance in the past three months.

_____ 2. I had a personal conversation with an unbeliever in the past two weeks.

_____ 3. I have at least three non-Christian friends.

_____ 4. I invited someone to a worship service or church-sponsored event in the past month.

_____ 5. I introduced myself to at least one visitor at a worship service in the past two weeks.

_____ 6. I prayed for my non-Christian friends and relatives last week.

_____ 7. I serve the Lord in at least one ministry within my congregation.

_____ 8. In the past month, I tried to help someone else begin to develop a world-class vision.

_____ 9. I showed love to someone outside my family in the past two weeks.

_____ 10. I'm acquainted with at least one local missionary or Christian outreach organization.

Total number of *yes* answers _____

10   Congratulations! Your nearsighted vision is almost perfect (well, nobody's perfect).

8–9   Your nearsightedness is better than most people's.

5–7   Good, you're trying.

2–4   You need to take a closer look at the people and needs around you.

0–1   Are you blind?

Biblical Texts to Study

- Acts 1:6–8

Things to Talk About

- Referencing the Scripture above, what geographic strategy of evangelization did Jesus outline to his disciples? How does Jesus' strategy apply to today's world?

- Why is it easier to be more concerned for the needs of other places and cultures than for the needs where we live?

- What evangelism tools are you aware of that present a clear gospel message? Identify several spiritually lost people in your world with whom you will share the gospel.

- Why is it important for world-class Christians to serve in their local congregations before serving the rest of the world?

- What are the local church's roles in missions, both local and international? What are some practical ways we can serve our churches in these roles?

- What are some needs in your local area, and in what practical ways can you serve them?

- On the Nearsightedness Test, choose one *no* answer that you will commit to making a *yes* in the next month. What steps will you take toward that goal?

GOD CALLS WORLDWIDE

Here am I. Send me!

THE PROPHET ISAIAH

It's frustrating to be given a responsibility to fulfill but no instruction on where to start.

In the earliest days of our church's short-term mission program, a team of young men from our church went to Whitehorse, in the Yukon Territories. They went to serve at the summer camp of a church and to help expand the camp facilities by building two log cabins.

When they arrived, the host was very busy, but he took some time one morning to show them the supplies, the logs, and the foundations on which the cabins were to be built. He directed them to a cabin that had already been completed and said, "When you're done, yours should look just like this one." Then he left. No drawings. No supervisor. No plans. All they had were the raw supplies and the work force—but they didn't know where to begin.

The team members floundered about for a day but finally realized they didn't know what they were doing. So they found the camp director and asked for help. An experienced builder visited with them for two hours, showing them the basics for building the log cabins, insulating the joints, and constructing the roofs. He gave them what they needed to get started.

We live in an interconnected world and in an age of global Christianity that invites us to live as world-class Christians. The church needs men and women who will open their eyes, hearts, and resources to pray for and serve our broken world. But many of us—who have the raw materials and energies—have no idea how to get started. We might desire to care for and be involved in our world, but we have no idea where to begin.

Sometime back, while encouraging students in my class to grow in their concern for the world, I quoted statistics with vigor, citing the number of hungry people in the world, of Muslims in Indonesia, and of churches persecuted by oppressive governments. I moved on to some facts about Burkina Faso in West Africa, when suddenly one of the students blurted out, "But I don't care about Burkina Faso!"

I was shocked. How could he be so calloused? As we talked afterward, however, I realized that I was the one in error. He was simply expressing his own frustration with the data I presented. It wasn't that he did not care about Burkina Faso or the people there; he simply didn't know *how to care*. He was saying, in effect, "But I cannot care about Burkina Faso. I don't know how to get started."

He knew what he was supposed to do, but he needed help investigating where God wanted him to dedicate his efforts.

Considering a Global Call?

As we grow in our knowledge of and commitment to the world, being involved with international students, giving sacrificially from our income, and witnessing to our neighbors may not be enough for us. We may need to step back and ask, "Is God saying to me, as he did in the presence of Isaiah, 'Whom shall I send? And who will go for us?'" (Isaiah 6:1–8). Are we willing to respond with an available spirit that says, "Here I am, Lord; send me. I'm open to considering your call into another culture"?

Al and Marilyn were on their way to a comfortable retirement when they heard a preacher challenge people to realize that Abraham was seventy-five years old when God called him out as the prototypical missionary (Genesis 12:1–4). The speaker continued, "And if you're under age seventy-five, don't think that God couldn't call you. His call into the world is not only for high schoolers and collegians. We don't stop asking about his call after age thirty. What about you?"

Al and Marilyn became early examples of an entire movement that has arisen across North America, the Finishers Project (www.finishers.org). Finishers are people of retirement or preretirement age who take into cross-cultural ministry their skills, financial freedom, and desire to serve (more on this later in the chapter). Al and Marilyn went on to serve Christ in Europe, using their organizational and linguistic skills accumulated through years of military and business experience. They sensed God calling them to something new, and rather than settle for a status quo retirement, they went. They illustrate that we should consider a global call as God prompts our spirits to do so—no matter what our age.

As we grow as world-class Christians, study the needs in other parts of the world, and befriend people from other cultures, those who observe us may respond, "Well, if you're so into the global advance of Christianity, what are you doing here in the United States?"

It's a good question. If we seek lifestyles that are credible with our Christian brothers and sisters, we need to take time to ask, "God, what about me? Am I where you want me long term? Should I consider overseas or cross-cultural service?" A global call may come for us simply as the logical outcome of our desire to live as world-class Christians.

Shortly before his death, the Christian musician Keith Green wrote a tract entitled, *Why YOU Should Go to the Mission Field.* In a song, Keith exhorts the body of Christ to consider worldwide service for a variety of reasons. His third reason says, "You should go because so few Christians are obeying the call, making the need [for international workers] even greater." He observes that Amway and Avon have fourteen times more representatives in the United States alone than the church of Jesus Christ has outside of the United States.

On a worldwide scale, Keith points out that while only 9 percent of the world speaks English, 94 percent of all ordained Christian preachers minister with the 9 percent who speak English. When he wrote that tract, there were an estimated 1 million full-time Christian workers in the United States. But at that time, one-half of the world's population (Muslims, Hindus, and Chinese) had only 2,417 Christian workers.[1] For Green, the inequities of the world were reason alone to consider if God were calling us to another land—for "how shall they hear without a preacher?" (Romans 10:14 KJV).

For many of us, a desire to be sensitive to and involved in God's global call might come simply because of the amazing times we live in. Philip Jenkins, condensing his book *The Next Christendom*, summarizes the situation:

The growth [of Christianity] in Africa has been relentless.

- In 1900, Africa had just 10 million Christians out of a continental population of 107 million—about 9 percent.
- Today the Christian total stands at 360 million out of 784 million, or 46 percent. And that percentage is likely to continue rising because Christian African countries have some of the world's most dramatic rates of population growth.

- Within the next twenty-five years, the population of the world's Christians is expected to grow to 2.6 billion (making Christianity by far the world's largest faith).
- By 2025, 50 percent of the Christian population will be in Africa and Latin America, and another 17 percent will be in Asia.
- By about 2050, the United States will still have the largest single contingent of Christians, but all the other leading nations will be Southern: Mexico, Brazil, Nigeria, the Democratic Republic of the Congo, Ethiopia, and the Philippines.[2]

Dr. Lamin Sanneh, originally a Muslim from the Gambia, West Africa, converted to Jesus Christ in his early adult years and is now a professor at Yale University. In his book *Whose Religion Is Christianity?* Sanneh highlights Christianity as the most global, transnational, and transcultural faith in the world.[3] The church is growing fastest in places like Africa, Asia, and Latin America.

If we listen to these leaders, we would consider God's global call because of the unique times in which we live. Indeed, the United States is roughly 5 percent of the world population. God is working globally, and he invites us to be a part.

But What's Available?

In spite of devout Christian parents and a strong personal commitment to Christ, Will had never considered cross-cultural service. When I asked him, he responded without defensiveness. He simply observed, "I cannot preach, translate the Bible, or do medical work, so it never entered my mind."

"What do you do?" I asked Will.

"I'm a construction worker," he answered. "I like to work with my hands."

"Then there are many places in the world you might go to serve. Perhaps you cannot translate, but if you joined Wycliffe Associates, you could build homes for people who can translate. Without people like you, translators would spend their time doing jobs they're not qualified to do."

Many of us understand Will's perspective because it's also ours. We think we have nothing to offer that would be useful in another culture or in an international setting. Before dismissing the possibility, however, consider the following truths about opportunities to serve the church around the world.

Opportunities: Mission Calls for Every Skill

More than ever before, a greater diversity of people and skills is needed in cross-cultural service. A city team from Latin America Mission needs a bookkeeper, a dental hygienist, a child psychologist, and a business manager. A traditional mission-sending agency listed the following international personnel needs and opportunities:

- a computer programmer and a web designer in Colombia
- an x-ray technician in Pakistan
- a biomedical technician in the United Arab Emirates
- a team secretary in France
- a librarian in Spain
- a teacher at an international school in Germany

The diversity of needs around the world makes it possible for almost anyone to consider a cross-cultural assignment in missions. A woman with grown children told me that her only qualification was her experience as a mother. I introduced her to the need for dorm parents at any number of schools for children of international workers. "If you become their surrogate mother while school is in session," I explained, "you'll be a partner with their parents, who may be serving with a tribe in some remote village."

The opportunities abound, and sometimes the nontraditional international worker has access to countries that do not allow conventional missionaries. One international agency executive writes, "In several locations around the world, medical personnel maintain the only officially permitted Christian witness. Agriculturists work with local people to develop more stable food supplies, creating a reservoir of goodwill. Educational specialists lecture in universities, teach technical skills, function as TESL (Teaching English as a Second Language) instructors, and staff schools that cannot employ enough local teachers."[4]

A single woman considers using her degree and experience in plant pathology to help in a reforestation project in West Africa. A lawyer goes to serve and defend the rights of the poor in the inner city. A veterinarian dedicates herself to helping with animal health in an agrarian society in Asia. A camp administrator looks into assisting the director of a Christian camp in Brazil. A television scriptwriter dedicates himself to Christian broadcasting in the Philippines.

The opportunities today make it possible for many to consider a variety of international service positions.

Opportunities: Short-Term Missions Join Service and Discovery

Short-term service opportunities offer a chance both to serve and to discover if we should go into another culture long term. When William Carey went to India in the late 1700s, short-term missions were out of the question. It took months to travel to foreign lands by boat, and when these first missionaries went, they worked in pioneering mission settings with people who may have been seeing Westerners for the first time.

Although pioneering situations still exist today, the world has changed drastically since William Carey went out. Jet air travel, the existence of the Christian church in many parts of the world, and an ever-increasing awareness of other cultures make short-term missions service possible. People now go across cultural barriers regularly for service opportunities that last from two weeks to three years.

As a result of short-term service projects in Burkina Faso, Turkey, and Egypt, Kristin entered college determined to prepare for international service. Her overseas experience confirmed her desire and ability to work cross-culturally. After college, she served in student ministry in France.

Eric attended our church as an average, twenty-five-year-old bookkeeper—until his two-week service project in Venezuela. On that trip, he met Christian workers who were just like him, and he saw opportunities to use his skills to assist ministries. After Venezuela, Eric served as bookkeeper and later as administrator in ministries serving the poor—leprosy patients in Liberia, relief and development work in Botswana, and small-business development (microfinance) in Slovakia.

Even Bob and Jean (whom I refer to later) started with eight days of serving in West Germany. Then they decided to spend a summer in short-term service at the Africa Inland Mission headquarters in Bristol, England. These two short-term experiences directed their steps and confirmed their call. Now they serve full-time in the international ministry of Campus Crusade for Christ.

A short-term ministry affords us the opportunity to meet needs in another culture while we simultaneously considering a long-term call.

Opportunities: Mission Calls for Tentmakers

Tentmaking introduces possibilities for outreach in countries that are closed to full-time Christian workers. Tetsunao Yamamori, president emeritus of Food for the Hungry and author of *God's New Envoys*, noted that 100,000 new envoys are needed to serve in countries closed to traditional missionaries.[5] These new envoys, "tentmakers," like Paul the apostle, use their secular skill to provide for their income (Acts 18:3). Tentmakers are often the only avenue for entrance into the countries where 90 percent of the world's unreached live.

Several years ago, Bart opened himself to the Lord in a new way. With his wife, he asked God to direct him in using his banking and leadership training to further God's kingdom. God led them toward North Africa, and after training, he and his family departed for a North African country that does not allow traditional Christian missionaries. Bart worked about twenty-five hours per week in a bank, enough to pay for their basic needs, and he dedicated the rest of his time to befriending Muslims and sharing the love of Christ with them.

Jack and his family served in Saudi Arabia, using his Ph.D. in molecular cell biology to teach at the university. Steve teaches English in China. Gene and Terry taught school to gain entrance to Nepal. Fred uses computer skills to serve in Malaysia. Many doors appear to be closing to conventional missionaries, but new doors are opening to those willing to use nontraditional means to gain entrance to these countries.

Mark Watney, formerly of the U.S. Center for World Mission, writes, "The missionary enterprise requires people from all professions. Nurses in a refugee camp in Pakistan, professors in a university in Shanghai, engineers in a consulting firm in Bahrain, or an English teacher in an adult school in East Los Angeles can all be tentmakers. Tentmakers are Christians who use their professions not for comfort and prestige, but to pry open unreached, poor, oppressed, and needy areas."[6]

Opportunities: Mission Calls for Retirees

New horizons of worldwide opportunity are open to those willing to serve in their retirement years. While in the military and then in private business, Al and Marilyn (referenced earlier) lived in Asia, Latin America, and Europe. Al speaks five languages; Marilyn, "only three." They're exceptional people—no matter where they might serve. But they chose to give their retirement years to serve in Europe.

Al and Marilyn serve as Finishers (discussed earlier), or "latter-day missionaries" (a phrase Al coined). Using retirement income and good health, they dedicated themselves to service internationally during the years many reserve for a leisure life in Florida.

Al and Marilyn do not serve alone. Bob and Jean (referenced earlier) retired early to serve in the international ministry of Campus Crusade. Using their years of experience in human resources, they serve the immense staff of Campus Crusade by helping to devise effective personnel policies.

Norm and Gladys use their retirement years to serve the staff of JAARS and Wycliffe Bible Translators. Using his computer experience and her nursing and administrative skills, they assist others around the world in the task of Bible translation.

International agencies find that increasing numbers of retirees desire to serve. As a result, many older men and women, who are at least partly financially independent, are discovering greater purpose in their retirement years than they ever thought possible.

But How?

Determining the will of God concerning cross-cultural service frightens us: How do I hear God's voice? Will he make me do something I absolutely detest?

There is no set formula for discovering God's will. Instead, consider this discovery as if viewing a constellation. When we look into the night sky, we need to see clusters of stars to view a constellation. Only by looking at the overall group of stars will we see Orion or the Big Dipper. Focusing on one star does not give us the big picture.

In the same way, discerning God's will involves looking at the big picture. When all of the "stars" come into view, we begin to understand the big picture that we call the personal will of God.

"Stars" that contribute to this big picture include the following:

- **Biblical guidance.** God will never ask us to do something contrary to his Word. He demands our obedience in the clearly revealed things; and obedience to his commission to make disciples may move us into cross-cultural service.

- **Opinion and counsel of others,** especially older, wise leaders who know us well. If many people commend us on our cross-cultural sensitivity and encourage us to pursue international service, maybe God is speaking through them.

- **Gifts and abilities.** God has entrusted us with certain unique personal resources. How will we use them?

- **Opportunities and situations.** If our company asks us to serve overseas or our church leaders invite us on a short-term mission trip, God might be speaking to us.

- **Desires.** A veteran missionary once told me that a desire to travel might be God's way of directing me toward service.

- **Initiative.** Taking steps of faith in one direction can help us affirm God's will as he either redirects us or confirms the direction we take. The Student Volunteer Movement taught that we should take steps toward cross-cultural service until God called us to stay home—"planning to go, but willing to stay."

- **Need.** While need is not the only star in the picture, it certainly shines brightly. God may use our knowledge of people without Jesus to compel us out. This certainly motivated Paul (Romans 15:20; 1 Corinthians 9:16–17), as well as many other great mission leaders in history. When Cam Townsend met people with no

Bible in their mother tongue, God called him to learn their language and translate the Bible. He later founded what is now Wycliffe Bible Translators.

- **Miraculous means.** In her book *God's Guidance: A Slow and Certain Light*, Elisabeth Elliot includes angels, dreams, audible and visible signs, and prophecies as ways that God guided in the Scriptures—and possibly how he might guide us today.[7]

What constitutes a cross-cultural or international call? The stars in the constellation vary, but after we get a clear picture from God, he calls us to obey.

Getting Started

Is God calling us into some type of cross-cultural service? We know what needs to be done, and workers are needed around the world. But how do we get started?

Three action steps may help us find where God might be calling us.

Step 1: Start Small

Malcolm Muggeridge writes, "Christianity is not a statistical view of life. That there should be more joy in heaven over one sinner who repents than over all the hosts of the just, is an anti-statistical proposition."[8] In other words, our little efforts do matter!

Todd and his friends decided they could not respond to the 20 million people living in Mexico City. But they could serve through Galo Vasquez by offering collateral for a no-interest loan program designed to help break the cycle of poverty. At the start, their efforts affected two or three families at the most—*but they got started.* As their ministry grew, a microfinance ministry developed, which is now self-sustaining (that is, receives no assistance from outside Mexico). "The Good Seed," the English translation of the ministry's name, now affects hundreds of families.

Our small efforts do matter. We belong to the God of the "mustard seed," who takes the smallest of actions and makes them significant in his economy (see Mark 4:30–32). Tom Sine writes in *The Mustard Seed Conspiracy*, "God has chosen to change the world through the lowly, the unassuming, and the imperceptible."[9]

Start small to investigate how we might be used to serve someone in our world.

Step 2: Start Here

Involvement with internationals, serving other cultures in our cities, or developing a second language skill can all take place without going overseas. Yet God can use these efforts to prepare us for something international.

Mr. and Mrs. Anderson decided to start building their world vision right at home. Each night they watch the network news together, but their growing world vision caused them to add a new response. They listen to the news, taking special note of the international reports. During the commercial breaks, they turn down the volume, and they pray together for the country or the issue that was cited. After praying about famine needs in North Africa, God led them there on an exploratory trip with World Vision.

Dick and Karen, at age fifty-seven, decided they should start right at home to explore the potential of serving overseas in their retirement years. They spent one year training in personal evangelism and another year training in cross-cultural adaptation. They have no firm direction yet, but they're making themselves available to serve God anywhere by starting here at home.

Step 3: Start Now

"These are good ideas. I'll have to try them out some day . . . when I have the time."

We'll never find where God might have us serve if we procrastinate and never ask. If we are to grow in our vision of God, his world, and our part in it, we need to make these our priorities. And we need to start today.

The first action we can take is to submit ourselves daily to the lordship of Christ. If we realize that we belong to him—"bought with a price" (1 Corinthians 6:20)—we will desire to grow in our ability to see the world as he sees it. Our desire to understand and care for our world will arise out of our relationship with Christ.

Lou and Donna are starting now to ask if God wants them to serve in another culture. In spite of the pressures of being young parents, they tell others, "If we say, 'Our lives are too hectic to evaluate where God might be calling us internationally,' we'll develop a pattern of running from that question for the rest of our lives. Life will always be hectic, so we need to open ourselves to God's worldwide plans for us now—even if we think we're in no position to respond."

Dr. Ralph Winter, the brilliant missions leader and founder of the U.S. Center for World Mission, stated, "Nothing that does not occur daily will ever dominate your life." If we don't start now to open ourselves to God as his living sacrifices (Romans 12:1), we may never hear him call us into an exciting opportunity to serve him worldwide.

Start small. Start here. Start now.

Biblical Texts to Study

- Acts 13

- Acts 9:26–29

- Acts 11:25–26

Things to Talk About

• Referencing the Scriptures above, how did Barnabas and Saul (later known as Paul) know that God was calling them into missionary service? Why were they chosen? What roles did the local church play in their missionary call and preparation?

• Identify other ways God might use to call us into cross-cultural service.

• What opportunities are available in missions today? How do these differ from missions in the past?

• Have you inquired, "God, what about me? Am I where you want me long term? Should I consider overseas service?" If so, what answer have you sensed from God?

• What education, skill, or experience do you have to offer? How might these be used in cross-cultural service?

• As we investigate ways God might use us in cross-cultural service, what are some practical ways to "start small, start here, and start now"?

13

YOU CAN BE A
WORLD-CLASS CHRISTIAN

No reserve. No retreat. No regrets.

WILLIAM BORDEN

My wife and I have tried to apply the principle of "living more simply" to our purchase of cars. We never purchase a brand-new model, and we have preferred "seasoned," older models. In light of the costs of the car, the excise tax, and the insurance rates in our state, older cars have saved us considerable amounts of money.

One car we purchased, a pumpkin-orange Volvo, had been driven over 100,000 miles. Nevertheless, it lasted for quite a while (we retired it with 172,000 miles). In its last winter, however, the mechanical problems intensified. The car would not start, so we called the tow truck. After the car had been in the shop for a few days, the mechanic told us, "I can get this baby started, but you'll never keep it going." We laid the car to rest in the junkyard.

When considering the incredible task of being world-class Christians, we feel like that old Volvo: We might get started, but can we keep going? "I can get my vision started. I can get excited about a few statistics, global issues, or praying for world missions. And every time I return home after serving on a short-term mission trip, I'm on fire to be a world-class Christian. But I'm never able to keep my vision going. I'm already worn out, so sustaining world-class Christian growth is beyond me."

How can we care about more than 1.3 billion people in China or the hungry in Latin America? None of us can fathom the vastness or the scope of God's total world mission, but we can start small and build our vision as part of our ongoing discipleship. In addition to increasing our appreciation for the awesomeness of the God we serve, a growing world vision will help us keep our personal problems in proper perspective.

The Going Won't Be Easy

"Why do we get such great attendance at our Christmas pageants but such dismal attendance at missions events?" The question stung. A concerned, internationally aware Christian was simply observing the obvious. I gave a few trite answers in immediate response, but his question made me think.

Was it because our presentations were shabby? Perhaps, but we'd been making concerted efforts to overcome this. Was it because our speakers were boring? Maybe, but even when we hosted top motivational speakers on the subject of global outreach, the turnout was still poor.

I finally realized that the focus of the two events was different. The Christmas pageant was musical, festive, and culturally acceptable. Although the gospel message was present, it came in the form of a celebration related to a popular holiday. The focal points for most were an innocent baby in a manger, peace, and goodwill.

In contrast, the essence of international, cross-cultural ministry is sacrifice. The gospel is obviously at the center, but in the form of cross-bearing unselfishness and giving. The Christmas pageant could satisfy those who came to receive. World-focused meetings were for those ready to give.

My evaluation forced me to realize that being a world-class Christian is truly countercultural. Asking for unselfishness, sacrifice, and Christlike service is foreign to a culture where our first question is often, "What's in this for me?"

Events that focus on international needs and cross-cultural service opportunities may never get the same type of attendance as concerts, Christmas pageants, or Easter services, but perhaps it's because the world-class Christian challenge has not been understood.

Building the Vision

Managerial experts frequently say, "Failing to plan is planning to fail." The saying holds true for our personal growth as world-class Christians. If we don't plan for expanding our vision by reading, praying, serving, and simple living, our growth probably will not happen.

To develop a growth plan, remember our definition of a world-class Christian: A world-class Christian is one whose lifestyle and obedience are compatible, in cooperation, and in accord with what God is doing and wants to do in our world. (See chapters 1, 2, and 3 for in-depth discussions on the meaning of the term *world-class Christian*.)

Keeping our vision going and growing means reading that definition slowly and asking, "Where are my strengths? Where are my weak spots? Where do I need to start growing?"

Each of us needs to grow in some aspect of that definition. So, let's review, putting together all we've learned into a vision-building plan.

Gaining the vision of a world-class Christian doesn't happen by accident. Seeing God's world as he sees it—with a world-class vision—begins with a specific plan to build, block by block, on the foundation of personal discipleship. The building may start small, but intentionally, persistently, and steadily we add vision-building blocks. As we've learned, critical vision-building blocks include the following:

- knowing God's world—by gathering *information*
- praying for God's world—through *intercession*
- living a credible lifestyle—through *integration* of our money and lifestyle into a world-class Christian vision
- being a doer in God's world—through practical *involvement*
- finding our place in God's mission—through *investigation* of God's call
- responding to God's call—by just doing it

As each block is laid, we will see more clearly, over time, God's world as he sees it, what God's doing in his world, what God wants to do in his world, and how we can cooperate with God in his kingdom-building work.

Here's a review of each vision-building block to be laid in our vision-building plan.

Building Block 1: Information

After our Sunday school class, a young man told me that he was going to commit himself that day to reading the international section of the newspaper. He said, "I usually read only the sports section, but I'm growing to understand that God may want to use that newspaper as my guide for prayer today."

A world-class vision cannot grow without fueling the vision with information. (See chapter 4 for an in-depth discussion on gathering information.) Here are sample goals for an individual or a study group to set for one month, six months, or a year.

- Learn geography: the countries of the world or perhaps the countries of one specific continent.

- Study the entire Bible to document God's commission to go into the whole world with the gospel.
- Read a book on missions theology, or read a specific missionary's biography.
- Attend an informational conference or seminar either on missions or on some issue in our world today.
- Do a personal research study on one country, culture, or issue of global concern, such as global warming, the church in China, globalization, or the rich-poor gap.
- Play a global-learning game (see Resources for Further Growth) to help your household grow in geographic knowledge.

The first building block for world-class growth is gathering information about God's world.

Building Block 2: Intercession

Prayer challenges our busy schedules because it takes time. Prayer also challenges our faith, because we may wrestle with doubts about the viability of prayer, asking ourselves, "What difference does it make?"

To build our vision for prayer, it's important to look again to the psalmist and realize that praising God for being the Lord of the whole earth is our starting point. Worship reminds us of the Lord of the harvest, and all the needs we bring before him take on perspective under him.

Many of the world's needs are so vast that we feel compelled to respond in prayer, committing needs to God when we can make no other response. I start almost every group meeting I lead by thanking God for the freedom we have to meet together as Christians. It's one small effort I can make to sensitize others and myself to Christians who suffer, sometimes for their faith, in other parts of our world.

We don't need to pray for the whole world, but we can expand our prayer horizons by adding one or two missions-related prayers to our daily intercession. (See chapters 5 and 6 for in-depth discussions on praying world-class prayers.)

Here are some suggested goals for building our faith and world-class vision through intercession.

- Use *Operation World* each week to start a Sunday school class or a weekly Bible study. Read the entry of the day, and ask one or two people to pray for that country.
- Study the prayers recorded in the Bible, paying special attention to what they teach about the character, mercy, and outreach of God.
- Watch the television news regularly, or read a weekly news magazine; then practice "arrow" prayers or "ever-widening circle" prayers for people or places in the news (see chapter 6).
- Read the biography of George Mueller to stimulate faith and conviction about prayer.
- Pray for one "people group" or country as you learn about it.

Paul exhorted the Thessalonians to "pray without ceasing" (1 Thessalonians 5:17 NASB). With a world before us, we will have plenty to "pray without ceasing" about.

The second building block for world-class growth is intercession for God's world.

Building Block 3: Integration

Jeff and Judy are newlyweds. They're also committed to grow in their world-class vision. As a result, they have determined that integration of that vision with daily life means avoiding the trap of accumulating things. "When you're first married," they observe, "you think to yourself, 'Wow, our apartment is so empty; we need this and we need that.' We've watched our married friends, and it takes no time at all to get bogged down with 'stuff.' As a result, we try to keep away from unnecessary purchases. God may send us to some developing country to serve, and we figure that it's good experience for us to get accustomed to living with less."

If we don't incorporate our world missions learning into our daily lives, missions will become mundane and irrelevant. We can start integrating a world-class vision into our lives by listening to international reports on the news, reading in *National Geographic* about places we don't know, and putting a world map above our desks. Christie and I integrate reminders of the great world into which we are called by surrounding ourselves with symbols of the greater world. A world map place mat, a desk blotter, a pencil sharpener, a clock, a paperweight, and even a beach ball set the world before us regularly. (See chapters 7 and 8 for in-depth discussions on the integrated lifestyle of a world-class Christian.)

Here are some suggested goals to keep the vision of an integrated lifestyle growing.

- Study in the Bible topics such as riches, stewardship, and management of resources.
- Read my book *Simplify: 106 Ways to Uncomplicate Your Life.*
- Increase your financial giving this month, even up to 1 percent.
- Find an overseas project to which your Bible study or Sunday school class can give an annual gift.
- Label the clothes hangers in your closet. The first time you wear the clothes, take the label off that hanger. After one year (or whatever amount of time you determine), give away the clothes on hangers that still have labels. If one year passes without us wearing a piece of clothing, perhaps someone else could use it more.
- Read Ronald Sider's book *Rich Christians in an Age of Hunger.*

- Buy clothes (you or your small group) to donate to a shelter for homeless people. (Shelters always need donations of new underwear.)
- Give something away!
- Read any of Tom Sine's books: *Mustard Seed Conspiracy*; *Why Settle for More and Miss the Best?*; and *Wild Hope*.
- Challenge yourself to avoid saying for one week or month, "I'm hungry," "I feel starved," or "I need . . ."
- Take a half day sometime over the next year to do a personal evaluation, asking questions such as "Where could I simplify my life?" "Am I being motivated by kingdom-of-God values or by materialistic values?" "How can I develop greater thankfulness for all I have?"

The third building block for world-class growth is living an integrated lifestyle.

Building Block 4: Involvement

"Give me something to do." The speaker, a young activist from our college group, desperately wanted to put what he had learned into practice. He wanted to be a doer of the Word, not merely a hearer (James 1:22).

As our vision for God's world grows, we need to find ways to respond practically. (See chapters 9 and 10 for in-depth discussions on being a doer of God's Word through practical involvement.)

Here are some world-vision-growing ways to get involved in God's diverse world.

- Get some training on how to share the gospel with friends and co-workers.
- Reach out to immigrants or international students in your community or nearby college; for example, organize a dinner for international students, held at

your church during a holiday (when they may be in the dormitories and most lonely).

- Participate in a service project at an inner-city ministry.
- Take your Sunday school class or Bible study group on a field trip into a new culture; for example, eat an international meal together, worship with a church from a different ethnic background, or serve some need in the community.
- Learn a few greetings in a language spoken by people who live nearby.
- Pray for and find ways to reach out in your community to subgroups that may usually be overlooked, such as the police, night-shift workers, the medical community.

The fourth building block for world-class growth is through practical involvement in God's world. Don't just stand there; do something!

Building Block 5: Investigation

As our vision grows, we will at some point have to wrestle with the questions: "What about me?" "Where do I fit?" "Where do I need to grow toward fulfilling God's design for me in this great world?" "Should I consider cross-cultural ministry?"

Opening ourselves to the lordship of Christ is basic to Christian growth. Perhaps he will call us into missions work, or he may direct us to stay right where we are. We'll never know without opening ourselves totally to him—and asking. (See chapters 11 and 12 for in-depth discussions on finding our place in God's mission through investigation of his call.)

Here are some possible goals for investigating our place in God's diverse world.

- Read a book on discerning the will of God: *God's Guidance: A Slow and Certain Light,* by Elisabeth Elliot or *Decision-Making by the Book,* by Haddon Robinson.
- Experiment with God's call by getting involved in a ministry and discovering if your gifts and abilities match the requirements.
- Look for opportunities to be a world-minded catalyst in your church, perhaps by joining (or starting) the international missions committee, by presenting the global challenge to others, or by giving others manageable tasks for learning and growing.
- Reevaluate your retirement plans now to determine how to spend your golden years in some sort of cross-cultural service.
- Read the S-H-A-P-E idea of discovering God's unique design for each of us, in Rick Warren's book *The Purpose-Driven Life.*
- Look into the need for "tentmakers" of your profession in limited-access countries. Could your profession help gain entry to a country where missionaries are not allowed?
- Ask others to help you discover your gifts and abilities.
- Commit your children and grandchildren to the Lord, even if that means their involvement in some international setting.

All of us have some part to play in God's worldwide plan, but it may take some serious investigation to discover exactly where he may want us in the days ahead.

The fifth building block for world-class growth is investigating God's call and our place in God's mission.

Just Do It

Growing as world-class Christians requires the discipline of exercise. In the same way that we combat the procrastination and excuses that keep us from jogging, biking, or swimming, we will need diligence to continue growing our world vision. The folks at Nike athletic shoes give us the exhortation we need. We know what needs to be done—JUST DO IT!

When I am prone to quit the task of making world-class growth a priority in my life, I remember people. I'm motivated by the changes I've seen in people as they opened their eyes to God's world and their hearts to God's service.

I remember . . .

> Bryan and Janet, who opened themselves to full-time ministry in a "second-career" phase of their lives because they have surrounded themselves with world-class Christian friends

> Marion, who chose to serve meals in Haiti rather than enjoy the rocking chair of retirement

> David, who uses his international business travel to encourage missionaries and national workers in the countries he visits

> Debbie and Norm, who started learning about India by inviting an Indian family to their home for their first taste of pizza

> Nathan, who at age five doesn't have a broad world vision, but he's learning to say "Africa" with excitement

Bob, who has worked out his own international vision by leading over fifteen service teams and by serving behind the scenes at our international student functions

All of these people have enlarged their vision for the world by investigating how God wanted to use them to have a global impact. These and dozens of others—changed by a greater view of God and his world—encourage me to continue toward the goal of being a world-class Christian.

In the 1800s, A. T. Pierson saw the Christian opportunity in his world as "a combination of grand opportunity and great responsibility; chance of glorious success or awful failure." Gordon Aeschliman observes that even greater opportunities are ahead:

> Never before has the shadow of the church been cast so far into distant places. Every tribe created by the hand of God now lives within the reach of Christians, be it through commerce, education, medicine, government, or neighborhood guilds.
>
> Our hour is unprecedented, our jungle is uncharted, our opportunities are unmatched. There is only one village left in our day, and it is called Planet Earth. To be a member of God's international family as humanity steps into the twenty-first century is perhaps the closest we'll get to heaven in the flesh.[1]

LET'S DO IT!

Things to Talk About

• What is the most important truth God taught you through this study? What is the most challenging truth?

- How have your attitudes changed toward world missions and your place in it?

- Identify some practical ways we can motivate others toward the "countercultural" lifestyle of a world-class Christian.

- Understanding the risks and challenges of a global vision, in what practical ways can we sustain and even expand our global vision?

My Global Growth Goals

Based on what you've learned from this book and on God's leading, set specific growth goals for the next year in each category below. Remember to make them manageable, bifocal, and practical. Let's just do it!

Information

Intercession

Integration

Involvement

Investigation

ONE HUNDRED EXTRAORDINARY WAYS TO PARTICIPATE IN GOD'S GLOBAL PURPOSE—BASED ON ACTS 1:8

Jerusalem

Reach out to people around you—of a similar socioeconomic or cultural/ethnic background.

1. Choose one or two neighbors or co-workers who don't know Jesus; pray for them by name every day.
2. Prayer-walk through your neighborhood, praying for every family and person to come to know Christ.
3. Get involved as a "fragrance of Christ" person in community activities (PTA, neighborhood associations, and so forth).
4. Offer a practical service to a family in need near you (car washing, lawn mowing).
5. Prayer-walk at your workplace: arrive early to pray over each desk, cubicle, office, and work area for people to come to know Christ.
6. Go to your local police department to ask how you can support them in prayer.
7. Take an evangelism course to learn how to share your faith.

8. Hold an open house simply to get to know your neighbors (hand deliver the invitations so that you make face-to-face contact).
9. Volunteer to read to children at a daycare center.
10. Invite your neighbors or co-workers to start a book club with you; then pray for opportunities to use popular books as a bridge to share the gospel.
11. Hold a garage sale; then donate the proceeds to a worthwhile local ministry.
12. Volunteer to chaperone public school events such as field trips, dances, or the prom.
13. Start a resale shop to collect used clothes, furniture, and appliances; then recycle them to local ministries or sell them to benefit local ministries.
14. Join or develop a ministry to hearing-impaired or other physically challenged people.
15. Establish a guest room in your house to entertain visitors or to help people in need of lodging during a job transition.
16. Start a weekly prayer meeting, along with other Christians, at your place of work.
17. Read a book on evangelism, such as *Becoming a Contagious Christian* by Hybels and Mittelburg.
18. Host a holiday party to get to know your neighbors.
19. Create a survey of questions designed to help you understand the spiritual perspectives of your neighbors; then offer a barbecue reward to thank them for participating.
20. Take a neighbor to lunch simply to get acquainted.
21. Host a "Great People of the Last 2000 Years" party, and invite people to watch the *Jesus* film.
22. Start an investigative, four-week Bible study at work or in your neighborhood, asking, "Who is Jesus?" by looking into the Gospel of John.

23. Invite your friends, neighbors, or co-workers to join you in "Samaria" or "ends of the earth" outreaches (below); sometimes people grow spiritually interested by serving.

24. Leave a piece of evangelistic literature for a waitperson—along with a generous tip.

25. Invite a friend to the movies; afterward, over coffee, try to understand your friend's outlook on life by discussing the movie.

Judea

Reach out to people in your own culture, but in the larger region.

26. Downsize your church or Christian group activities, especially if you're involved three or more nights of the week; instead, get involved in the community—join a club, take a course, join a team.

27. Organize a Christmas toy drive to collect toys for underprivileged children in your area.

28. Take a course at a local university in philosophy, world religions, or some other subject that could provoke evangelistic conversations.

29. Volunteer at a church-centered conference that is dedicated to helping local churches become more effective in outreach, for example a Saddleback Church conference or Willow Creek's Leadership Summit.

30. Start a file of newspaper articles on a specific concern in your community that you want to make a focus of prayer or involvement.

31. Attend the training and then volunteer as a counselor for the Billy Graham crusade in your area (or some other televised crusade).

32. Run for office on the school committee or some other significant community leadership position.

33. Get involved in regional outreaches, joining with other churches to affect the community.

34. Write or call political leaders in the county government concerning an issue about which you're concerned.

35. Call a radio talk show to offer a Christian influence in conversations of local concern.

36. Get involved in (or start) a local food pantry for underprivileged families.

37. Volunteer at a local crisis-pregnancy center or hot line.

38. Organize an evangelistic dinner in your area for people of your profession; have a Christian from your profession speak.

39. Write a letter to encourage local political leaders and to offer your prayer support.

40. Visit once or twice each month lonely residents in local long-term care facilities or nursing homes.

41. Clean the public restrooms in your community.

42. Help in a ministry to alcohol- or chemically addicted people.

43. Volunteer in projects to "spruce up" your community (plant flowers, rake leaves, paint).

44. Buy food vouchers from a local restaurant to give to homeless people who approach you for money.

45. Obtain a list of area school principals to pray regularly for these key leaders.

46. Collect loose coins throughout the month; then donate the sum to local Christian ministries.

47. Get involved in efforts to prevent spouse or child abuse in your community.

48. Support the evangelistically oriented programs of local Christian radio programs.

49. Organize a clothing drive in your area; then donate the clothes to a city ministry to the homeless.

50. Memorize Luke 19:10; then create a list of the potential "lost" people you'd like to reach in your area.

Samaria

Reach out across cultures, but near to home—geographically close, but culturally distant.

51. Visit an ethnic restaurant to engage the owners in conversation about their country of origin, their culture, and their faith.
52. Become a host family for the international student ministry at your local university.
53. Volunteer to serve each month at a shelter for the homeless.
54. Buy products that are sold to benefit a local need-relief ministry.
55. Teach at a local English-as-a-second-language program (ESL).
56. Collect and donate Christmas presents to Prison Fellowship (or another prison ministry), which distributes gifts to the children of inmates.
57. Volunteer at an urban ministry to tutor students working toward a GED (graduate equivalency degree).
58. Visit a church that worships in a language different from your own in order to better comprehend the international nature of the body of Christ.
59. Start a pen pal ministry to prisoners at a local correctional facility.
60. Ask the local school administrator what languages are spoken in your neighborhood schools.
61. Invite a first-generation American co-worker to your home for a meal.
62. Become a "big brother" or "big sister" to a child with only one parent.
63. Get involved in a weekly or monthly prison-outreach ministry or an on-site Bible study.
64. Visit and get to know local ministries serving in ways that are "cross-cultural" to you (ministry with gangs or with HIV/ AIDS patients).

65. Prayer-walk in cross-cultural urban areas.

66. Visit leaders of a Muslim mosque, Hindu temple, or Buddhist temple in an effort to understand what other religions believe and teach.

67. Identify one project each month you can do for the people in need listed by Jesus in Matthew 25 (hungry, naked, lonely, and others).

68. Attend a local cultural or ethnic event in an effort to understand the cultures in your area.

69. Memorize 1 John 3:16–18.

70. Attend a class or seminar that trains in cultural understanding.

71. Develop your own "welcome wagon" ministry to newly arrived immigrants in your community, helping them with shopping, driving, or daily routines.

72. "Hang out" in the ethnic food section of your supermarket, asking God to help you meet people.

73. Invite people from other cultures to discuss with you this question: What is a Christian?

74. Raise money to take a group of underprivileged kids to a sporting event.

75. Live in the inner city for a weekend with an urban friend.

Ends of the Earth

Reach out to the ends of the earth—international outreach.

76. Pray for the country on the label of your clothing.

77. Buy a copy of *Operation World* to use as your reference book for praying for the nations of the world.

78. Post in a prominent place an up-to-date map of the world to provoke you to pray.

79. Listen to the BBC or other world news report; then pray for the countries mentioned.

80. Read a book on religions of the world.

81. Pray daily for one "adopted" country (other than your own).

82. Pray for one week for the Muslim countries in North Africa, the Middle East, South Asia, and especially the world's largest Muslim country, Indonesia.

83. Fast regularly; donate the money saved for ministry to the world's starving people (Isaiah 58:6–7).

84. Look into short-term mission opportunities (one or two weeks) to another part of the world.

85. Learn a foreign language (or at least some greetings or phrases in locally spoken languages).

86. Host someone who works internationally in your home, and learn about his or her work.

87. Memorize Acts 1:8.

88. Organize a fundraiser (a marathon or other event) to raise money for ministries dedicated to serving the world's poor or hungry.

89. Pray daily for an influential world leader whom you want to come to know Jesus Christ.

90. Pray for one week for the world's largest Hindu countries, India and Nepal.

91. Evaluate your budget to find $25 per month to adopt a child through World Vision, Compassion International, or some other Christian ministry to children.

92. Call a missionary or an international Christian worker you know simply to offer prayer and encouragement.

93. Pray for the Lord to raise up laborers (Matthew 9:36–38) to the peoples of the earth who have no knowledge of Jesus Christ.

94. Look ahead to your retirement for someplace in the world you could serve using your accumulated experience and skills.

95. Memorize Matthew 28:18–20.

96. Get involved in evangelistic outreaches at sporting events that involve international teams.

97. Pray for God's Word to go forward in the world's most populous nation, China, with over 1.3 billion people.

98. Organize a prayer meeting to pray for five or six foreign countries (spice it up by asking people to bring international foods).

99. Pray for your children to be open to wherever God might call them in service to his world.

100. Look into a three- to six-month leave of absence from your work to serve in another country.

NOTES

Chapter One

1. Howard Foltz, *Missions Link* 1, no. 7 (August 1989): 1.

2. Chapter 2 in this volume will define the term *world-class* as it applies to Christians. It refers not to the ability to "compete" worldwide, but to the qualities of faith that are compatible, in cooperation, and in accord with what God wants to do through his people in this world.

3. Tom Sine, "Will the Real Cultural Christian Please Stand Up?" *World Vision* (October/November 1989): 21.

4. With respect to Christian involvement in environmental issues, see Brown, *Our Father's World.*

5. "Lord of the Universe, Hope of the World" was the theme of InterVarsity's Urbana Student Missions Convention in 1990.

6. The term *Great Commission* refers to the final mandate of Jesus (recorded in various forms in Matthew 28:18–20; Mark 16:15; Luke 24:47; John 20:21; and Acts 1:8); a generally accepted definition summarizes the mandate as "making disciples of all nations." When this Great Commission is accomplished, most scholars believe it will prepare us for the second coming of Jesus (Matthew 24:14).

Chapter Two

1. Gordon Aeschliman, "Dancing on the Shrinking Globe," *World Christian* (May 1990): 9.

Chapter Three

1. Oswald Chambers, *My Utmost for His Highest* (New York: Dodd, Mead and Company, 1935), 288.

2. See Exodus 22:21; Leviticus 19:33–34; and Deuteronomy 10:17–19. These verses in the Law teach that the people of Israel were to love the lowly, the alien, and the stranger because the Israelites had themselves been aliens in Egypt.

3. Quoted from the World Vision International Christmas card (1989).

4. At the close of each Gospel and in Acts 1, we have a varied form of Jesus' Great Commission: Matthew 28:18–20; Mark 16:15; Luke 24:47; John 20:21; and Acts 1:8.

5. Chambers, *My Utmost,* 265.

6. Quote found in Winter and Hawthorne, *Perspectives on the World Christian Movement* (1981), 9.

7. Many of these stories are found in Tucker, *From Jerusalem to Irian Jaya.*

8. Jacobs, *Black Americans and the Missionary Movement in Africa,* 51.

9. Floyd McClung relates this story in *Living on the Devil's Doorstep.*

Chapter Four

1. Brian F. O'Connell, "Understanding Your World," *Discipleship Journal* 41 (1987): 18.

2. "Geography: Greek to Young Americans," The Associated Press (May 2, 2006). Reported by CNN.

3. Louis Wigdor, "Taking Global Education Seriously," *The Common Wealth* (Fall 1989): 1–2.

4. Ibid., 2.

5. Anagrams by Beatrice Bachrach Perri. Answers: (1) Lisbon, (2) Madrid, (3) Helsinki, (4) Paris, (5) Tirana, (6) Prague, (7) Belgrade, (8) Warsaw, (9) Bucharest, (10) Copenhagen, (11) Athens, and (12) London.

6. Watkins, *Seven Worlds to Win,* 9–183.

7. Scott Wesley Brown, "Look What God Is Doing," from the album *To the Ends of the Earth* (Word Records, 1988).

Chapter Five

1. K. P. Yohannan, founder of Gospel for Asia, a ministry dedicated to mobilizing evangelists and church planters in the Indian subcontinent, speaks to the matter of God's sovereign power and mercy when he challenges his American audiences. He observes, "In light of global needs and opportunities, and in light of the biblical teaching that unto whom much is given is much required, every Christian in the United States needs to ask, 'Why did God allow me to be born here?'"

2. Lawrence, *The Church in China,* 117.

3. Ibid.

4. Wells, *A Vision for Missions,* 138.

5. James Reapsome, "What's Holding Up World Evangelization? The Church Itself," *Evangelical Missions Quarterly* (April 1988): 117.

6. *Reader's Digest* (January 1986): 171.

7. Duewel, *Touch the World through Prayer,* 186–7.

Chapter Six

1. Howard, *The Great Commission for Today,* 98–102.

2. Some of these suggestions appeared in my article "Around the World on Your Knees," *Discipleship Journal* 48 (1988): 10.

3. Quote from *How to Pray for Your Missionaries*, a brochure published by Greater Europe Mission.

4. Caleb Resources, "Prayer Tips: Praying for the Unreached," *Co-Laborer* (Fall 1989).

5. Portions of this chapter appeared in my article "Sharpen Your Global Prayers," *World Vision* (August/September 1989, HM1).

Chapter Seven

1. Judith Viorst, *Alexander and the Terrible, Horrible, No Good, Very Bad Day* (New York: Simon and Schuster, 1987).

2. Tom Sine, "Right-Side-Up Values in an Upside-Down World: Whole-Life Discipleship in the '90s," *Discipleship Journal* 55 (1990): 37.

3. Patrick Johnstone, "The Cost of Evangelizing the World," *Alliance Life* 3 (January 1990): 7.

4. Helpful resources for managing money effectively include resources written by Ron Blue or Dave Ramsey, the Good Sense training materials generated by the Willow Creek Association, and Borthwick, *Simplify: 106 Ways to Uncomplicate Your Life*.

5. Tom Sine, "Will the Real Cultural Christians Please Stand Up?" *World Vision* (October/November 1989): 21.

6. Scott Wesley Brown, "Things," from the album *To the Ends of the Earth* (Word Records, 1988).

Chapter Eight

1. Perhaps the most thorough biblical study on money, possessions, and wealth is Blomberg, *Neither Poverty nor Riches*.

2. C. S. Lewis, *Mere Christianity* (New York: Macmillan, 1958), 81–82.

3. Haddon Robinson, *Mastering Contemporary Preaching* (Portland, OR: Multnomah, 1989), 105.

4. Tom Sine, "Shifting Stewardship into the Future Tense," *NAE Action* (March/April 1990): 11.

5. Robinson, *Mastering Contemporary Preaching*, 110–11.

Chapter Nine

1. Appleby, *Missions Have Come to America*, 8–9.

2. Lau, *The World at Your Doorstep*, 12–13.

3. Kathy Lay, "International Outreach," *Today's Christian Woman* (September 1989): 85.

4. Thomas, *Faces in the Crowd*.

5. Gordon Loux, "Reach the World from Your Living Room," *World Vision* (February/March 1990): 11.

6. Adapted from a list by Joy Cordell, "How to Launch a Foreign Friendship," *World Vision* (February/March 1990): 11.

7. Mark Rente, "Diplomats in Our Backyard," *Newsweek* (February 16, 1987): 10.

8. Nate Mirza quoted this from *The Baptist Standard* (June 28, 1989).

Chapter Ten

1. Roberts, *Glocalization.*

2. Tournier, *The Adventure of Living,* 153.

3. Angee Walsh, "How to Be a Foreign Missionary . . . Without Leaving Home," *Moody Monthly* (December 1988): 29–33.

4. Tom Sine, "Shifting into the Future Tense," *Christianity Today* (November 1989): 21.

5. John Perkins, "The Danger of a Homogeneous Fellowship," *World Christian* (May 1990): 18.

6. Diane Eble, "Making a Difference," *Campus Life* (May 1988): 42.

7. "Globe-Hopping Mama," *First* (December 1989): 5.

8. Noted in an article by Jerry Butler, "International Ministries," *Willow Creek* (November/December 1989): 27.

9. "Where in the World!" *Paraclete* 1 (U.S. Center for World Mission newsletter): 11.

10. Chris Eaton, "Short-Term Missions for Single Adults: Why and How," *Single Adult Ministries Journal* (February 1988): 3.

11. Quoted in Poyner, *From the Campus to the World,* 151.

12. Dale Hanson Bourke, "Better Off in Guatemala," *Today's Christian Woman* (January/February 1990): 72.

13. Ibid.

Chapter Eleven

1. Paul A. Beals, *A People for His Name* (Grand Rapids, MI: Baker, 1988), 9.

2. Some of the following material is adapted from my article "Overcoming Missions Malaise," *Leadership* (Winter 1988): 88–94.

3. James Reapsome, "Great Commission Deadline," *Christianity Today* (January 15, 1988): 27.

4. Ibid.

5. Kane, *Wanted: World Christians!* 105.

Chapter Twelve

1. Keith Green, *Why YOU Should Go to the Mission Field* (Last Days Ministries, 1982).

2. Philip Jenkins, "The Next Christianity," *Atlantic Monthly* (October 2002): 55, 58; the article summarizes Jenkins, *The Next Christendom.*

3. Sanneh, *Whose Religion Is Christianity?*

4. Donald K. Smith, "The Many Faces of Missions," *Impact* (February 1990): 13.

5. Yamamori, *God's New Envoys,* 58.

6. Mark Watney, "Wanted: 100,000 New Envoys," *The Caleb Project Newsletter* (February 1990): 3.

7. Elliot, *God's Guidance.*

8. Muggeridge, *Something Beautiful for God*, 81.

9. Sine, *The Mustard Seed Conspiracy*, 23.

Chapter Thirteen

1. Gordon Aeschliman, "Dancing on the Shrinking Globe," *World Christian* (May 1990): 9.

RESOURCES FOR FURTHER GROWTH

Looking outward—developing a bigger view of the world—is an essential part of our continued world-class growth. The following books, geography learning games, and organization websites can help us stay outwardly oriented, conscious of our world, and equipped to find our place in God's global plan.

Books

Appleby, Jerry L. 1986. *Missions Have Come to America.* Kansas City: Beacon Hill.

Barrett, David B., George T. Kurian, and Todd M. Johnson, eds. 2001. *World Christian Encyclopedia.* New York: Oxford.

Beals, Paul A. 1999. *A People for His Name.* Pasadena, CA: William Carey Library (revised).

Bediako, Kwame. 1997. *Christianity in Africa.* Maryknoll, NY: Orbis.

Blomberg, Craig L. 2001. *Neither Poverty nor Riches: A Biblical Theology of Possessions.* Downers Grove, IL: InterVarsity.

Borthwick, Paul. 1987. *A Mind for Missions.* Colorado Springs: NavPress.

———. 1996. *Six Dangerous Questions to Transform Your View of the World.* Downers Grove, IL: InterVarsity.

———. 2000. *Missions: God's Heart for the World.* Downers Grove, IL: InterVarsity.

———. 2003. *Stop Witnessing . . . and Start Loving.* Colorado Springs: NavPress.

———. 2006. *Youth and Missions.* Colorado Springs: Authentic.

―――. 2007. *Simplify: 106 Ways to Uncomplicate Your Life.* Colorado Springs: Authentic.

Bosch, David J. 1991. *Transforming Mission: Paradigm Shifts in Theology of Mission.* Maryknoll, NY: Orbis.

Brown, Edward R. 2008. *Our Father's World: Mobilizing the Church to Care for Creation.* Downers Grove, IL: InterVarsity.

Campolo, Tony. 2003. *You Can Make a Difference!* Nashville: Thomas Nelson.

Conde-Frazier, Elizabeth, S. Steve Kang, and Gary A. Parrett. 2004. *A Many Colored Kingdom.* Grand Rapids, MI: Baker.

Corduan, Winfried. 1998. *Neighboring Faiths.* Downers Grove, IL: InterVarsity.

DeYoung, Emerson, Yancey, and Kim. 2004. *United by Faith: The Multiracial Congregation as an Answer to the Problem of Race.* New York: Oxford.

Duewel, Wesley L. 1986. *Touch the World through Prayer.* Grand Rapids, MI: Zondervan.

Dyrness, William. 1998. *Let the Earth Rejoice!* Eugene, OR: Wipf and Stock.

Elliot, Elisabeth. 1997. *God's Guidance: A Slow and Certain Light.* Grand Rapids, MI: Revell.

―――. 2005. *A Chance to Die: The Life and Legacy of Amy Carmichael.* Grand Rapids, MI: Revell.

―――. 2008. *Shadow of the Almighty: The Life and Testament of Jim Elliot.* Peabody, MA: Hendrickson.

Engle, James F., and William A. Dyrness. 2000. *Changing the Mind of Missions: Where Have We Gone Wrong?* Downers Grove, IL: InterVarsity.

Escobar, Samuel. 2003. *The New Global Mission: The Gospel from Everywhere to Everyone.* Downers Grove, IL: InterVarsity.

Fernando, Ajith. 2001. *Sharing the Truth in Love.* Grand Rapids, MI: Discovery House.

Friedman, Thomas L. 2000. *The Lexus and the Olive Tree: Understanding Globalization.* New York: Farrar, Straus, and Giroux.

Global Prayer Digest. Published monthly by the U.S. Center for World Mission. http://www.uscwm.org.

Griffiths, Michael. 1993. *Give Up Your Small Ambitions.* Nashville: Accelerated Christian Education, Inc.

Guder, Darrell L. 1998. *Missional Church: A Vision for the Sending of the Church in North America.* Grand Rapids, MI: Eerdmans.

Guthrie, Stan. 2005. *Missions in the Third Millennium.* Colorado Springs: Paternoster.

Harris, Paula, and Doug Schaupp. 2004. *Being White: Find Our Place in a Multiethnic World.* Downers Grove, IL: InterVarsity.

Hoke, Steve, and Bill Taylor. 1999. *Send Me! Your Journey to the Nations.* Seattle: World Evangelical Alliance.

Hopler, Thom, and Marcia Hopler. 1994. *Reaching the World Next Door.* Downers Grove, IL: InterVarsity.

Howard, David. 1976. *The Great Commission for Today.* Downers Grove, IL: InterVarsity.

Hunter, George G. 1992. *How to Reach Secular People.* Nashville: Abingdon.

Hybels, Bill, and Mark Mittelburg. 1996. *Becoming a Contagious Christian.* Grand Rapids, MI: Zondervan.

Jacks, Bob, Matthew R. Jacks, and Pam Mellskog. 2006. *Divine Appointments.* Colorado Springs: NavPress.

Jacobs, Sylvia M., ed. 1982. *Black Americans and the Missionary Movement in Africa.* Westport, CT: Greenwood.

Jenkins, Philip. 2007. *The Next Christendom.* New York: Oxford (revised).

———. 2008. *The New Faces of Christianity: Believing the Bible in the Global South.* New York: Oxford.

Johnstone, Patrick. 1998. *The Church Is Bigger Than You Think: The Unfinished Work of World Evangelization.* Geanies House, Fearn, Scotland: Christian Focus.

———, and Jason Mandryk. 2005. *Operation World.* Colorado Springs: Authentic (revised).

Kaiser, Walter. 2000. *Mission in the Old Testament.* Grand Rapids, MI: Baker.

Kane, J. Herbert. 1986. *Wanted: World Christians!* Grand Rapids, MI: Baker.

Kirk, J. Andrew. 2000. *What Is Mission? Theological Explorations.* Minneapolis: Augsburg Fortress.

Kostenberger, Andreas J., and Peter T. O'Brien. 2001. *Salvation to the Ends of the Earth.* Downers Grove, IL: InterVarsity.

Lau, Lawson. 1984. *The World at Your Doorstep.* Downers Grove, IL: InterVarsity.

Lawrence, Carl. 1985. *The Church in China.* Minneapolis: Bethany.

McClung, Floyd. 1999. *Living on the Devil's Doorstep.* Seattle: YWAM.

———, and Kalafi Moala. 1989. *Nine Worlds to Win.* Colorado Springs: Authentic.

McNeil, Brenda Salter, and Rick Richardson. 2009. *The Heart of Racial Justice.* Downers Grove, IL: InterVarsity.

McQuilkin, J. Robertson. 2002. *The Great Omission.* Colorado Springs: Authentic.

Mittelburg, Mark. 2007. *Becoming a Contagious Church.* Grand Rapids, MI: Zondervan.

Moreau, Scott, Gary R. Corwin, and Gary B. McGee. 2004. *Introducing World Mission.* Grand Rapids, MI: Baker.

Muggeridge, Malcolm. 1971. *Something Beautiful for God.* New York: Harper and Row.

Myers, Bryant L. 2003. *Exploring World Mission.* Federal Way, WA: World Vision.

Newbigin, Lesslie. 1989. *The Gospel in a Pluralistic Society.* Grand Rapids, MI: Eerdmans.

Olson, Bruce. 2006. *Bruchko.* Lake Mary, FL: Charisma House.

Operation World Prayer Calendar. 2001. Colorado Springs: Authentic.

Ortiz, Manuel. 1996. *One New People: Models for Developing a Multiethnic Church.* Downers Grove, IL: InterVarsity.

Padilla, C. René. 1985. *Mission Between the Times: Essays on the Kingdom.* Grand Rapids, MI: Eerdmans.

Peart, Norman Anthony. 2000. *Separate No More: Understanding and Developing Racial Reconciliation in Your Church.* Grand Rapids, MI: Baker.

Peskett, Howard, and Vinoth Ramachandra. 2003. *The Message of Missions.* Downers Grove, IL: InterVarsity.

Piper, John. 2003. *Let the Nations Be Glad.* Grand Rapids, MI: Baker.

Pippert, Rebecca Manley. 1999. *Out of the Saltshaker and into the World.* Downers Grove, IL: InterVarsity.

Pollock, John. 2008. *Hudson Taylor and Maria.* Geanies House, Fearn, Scotland: Christian Focus.

Poyner, Alice. 1983. *From the Campus to the World.* Downers Grove, IL: InterVarsity.

Ramachandra, Vinoth. 2000. *Faiths in Conflict: Christian Integrity in a Multicultural World.* Downers Grove, IL: InterVarsity.

Raymo, Jim. 1996. *Marching to a Different Drummer: Rediscovering Missions in an Age of Affluence and Self-Interest.* Fort Washington, PA: Christian Literature Crusade.

Rhodes, Stephen A. 1998. *Where the Nations Meet: The Church in a Multicultural World.* Downers Grove, IL: InterVarsity.

Richardson, Don. 2006. *Eternity in Their Hearts.* Ventura, CA: Regal Books.

———. 2008. *Lords of the Earth*. Ventura, CA: Regal Books.

Richardson, Rick. 2000. *Evangelism Outside the Box*. Downers Grove, IL: InterVarsity.

Roberts, Bob Jr. 2007. *Glocalization: How Followers of Jesus Engage a Flat World*. Grand Rapids, MI: Zondervan.

Robinson, Haddon. 1998. *Decision-Making by the Book*. Grand Rapids, MI: Discovery House.

Roseveare, Helen. 2006. *He Gave Us a Valley*. Geanies House, Fearn, Scotland: Christian Focus.

Sanneh, Lamin. 2003. *Whose Religion Is Christianity?* Grand Rapids, MI: Eerdmans.

———. 2008. *Translating the Message: The Missionary Impact on Culture*. Maryknoll, NY: Orbis.

Sider, Ronald. 2005. *Rich Christians in an Age of Hunger*. Nashville: Thomas Nelson.

Sine, Tom. 1978. *The Mustard Seed Conspiracy*. Waco, TX: Word.

———. 1989. *Why Settle for More and Miss the Best?* Colorado Springs: Paternoster.

———. 1991. *Wild Hope*. Waco, TX: Word.

Spencer, Aída Besançon, and William David Spencer, eds. 1998. *The Global God: Multicultural Evangelical Views of God*. Grand Rapids, MI: Baker.

Stackhouse, Max L., Tim Dearborn, and Scott R. Paeth, eds. 2005. *The Local Church in a Global Era*. Eugene, OR: Wipf and Stock.

Stearns, Bill, and Amy Stearns. 2005. *2020 Vision: Amazing Stories of What God Is Doing Around the World*. Minneapolis: Bethany.

Stott, John. 1985. *Involvement: Being a Responsible Christian in a Non-Christian Society*, vol. 1; *Social and Sexual Relationships in the Modern World*, vol. 2. Old Tappan, NJ: Revell.

———. 1990. *The Spirit, the Church, and the World: The Message of Acts*. Downers Grove, IL: InterVarsity.

———. 2009. *Christian Mission in the Modern World*. Downers Grove, IL: InterVarsity.

Strobel, Lee. 1998. *The Case for Christ*. Grand Rapids, MI: Zondervan.

Taylor, Dr. and Mrs. Howard. 2008. *Hudson Taylor's Spiritual Secret*. Peabody, MA: Hendrickson.

The Global P.E.A.C.E. Plan, Saddleback Church. http://www.thepeaceplan.com.

The Kneeling Christian. 2006. Author unknown. Peabody, MA: Hendrickson.

Thomas, Donna. 2008. *Faces in the Crowd: Reaching Your International Neighbor for Christ.* Birmingham, AL: New Hope.

Tournier, Paul. 1963. *The Adventure of Living.* New York: Harper and Row.

Tucker, Ruth. 1988. *Guardians of the Great Commission.* Grand Rapids, MI: Zondervan.

———. 2004. *From Jerusalem to Irian Jaya.* Grand Rapids, MI: Zondervan.

Tutu, Desmond. 1992. *No Future Without Forgiveness.* New York: Doubleday.

———. 1994. *The Rainbow People of God.* New York: Doubleday.

Twiss, Richard. 2000. *One Church, Many Tribes.* Ventura, CA: Regal Books.

Van Engen, Charles E. 1991. *God's Missionary People: Rethinking the Purpose of the Local Church.* Grand Rapids, MI: Baker.

———. 1996. *Mission on the Way: Issues in Mission Theology.* Grand Rapids, MI: Baker.

Walls, Andrew F. 2002. The Ephesian Moment. In *The Cross-Cultural Process in Christian History.* Maryknoll, NY: Orbis.

Warren, Rick. 2002. *The Purpose-Driven Life: What on Earth Am I Here For?* Grand Rapids, MI: Zondervan.

Watkins, Morris. 1987. *Seven Worlds to Win.* Fullerton, CA: R. C. Law.

Wells, Tom. 1985. *A Vision for Missions.* Carlisle, PA: Banner of Truth.

Winter, Ralph, and Steven C. Hawthorne, eds. 2009. *Perspectives on the World Christian Movement.* Pasadena, CA: William Carey Library.

Yamamori, Tetsunao. 1988. *God's New Envoys.* Portland, OR: Multnomah.

Yancey, George. 2003. *One Body, One Spirit: Principles of Successful Multiracial Churches.* Downers Grove, IL: InterVarsity.

Yohannan, K. P. 2004. *Revolution in World Missions.* Carrollton, TX: Gospel for Asia.

Geography Learning Games

www.learninggamesforkids.com/geography_games.html

www.sheppardsoftware.com/web_games.htm

www.ilike2learn.com/ilike2learn/

www.familygames.com/share/wgt.html

www.resourcegames.com

Organization Websites

African Inland Mission International
www.aim-us.org

Arab World Ministries
www.awm.org

Bread for the World
www.bread.org

Campus Crusade for Christ International
www.ccci.org

Child Evangelism Fellowship
www.cefonline.com

ChristianJobs.com
www.christianjobs.com

Compassion International
www.compassion.com

Development Associates International
www.daintl.org

English Language Institute
www.elic.org

Finishers Project
www.finishers.org

Food for the Hungry International
www.fhi.net

Frontiers
www.frontiers.org

Global P.E.A.C.E. Plan, The
www.thepeaceplan.com

Greater Europe Mission
www.gemission.org

HCJB Global
www.hcjb.org

International Fellowship of Evangelical Students
www.ifesworld.org

International Justice Mission
www.ijm.org

International Students, Inc. (ISI)
www.isionline.org

InterVarsity Christian Fellowship
www.intervarsity.org

Joshua Project
www.joshuaproject.net

Lausanne Congress for World Evangelization, The
www.lausanne.org

Mission Exchange, The
www.missionexchange.org

Mustard Seed Associates
www.msainfo.org

National Geographic Society
www.nationalgeographic.com

Operation Mobilization
www.usa.om.org

Operation World
www.operationworld.org

Overseas Missionary Fellowship (OMF)
www.omf.org

Partners International
www.partnersintl.org

Prison Fellowship
www.prisonfellowship.org

SEND International
www.send.org

Perspectives on the World Christian Movement course,
    U.S. Center for World Mission
www.uscwm.org

SIM International
www.sim.org

Urbana Student Missions Convention
www.urbana.org

Walk for Hunger, The
www.projectbread.org

World Evangelical Alliance
www.worldevangelicals.org

World Relief
www.wr.org

World Vision
www.wvi.org

Wycliffe Bible Translators
www.wycliffe.org

Youth With A Mission (YWAM)
www.ywam.org